Fresh Ideas

with *Leigh Ann*

Fresh Ideas
with *Leigh Ann*

The Fred Meyer Cookbook

By Leigh Ann Hieronymus

Concept by Greg Mowery

Edited by Katherine Miller

Carpe Diem Books®

Text and photography © 2014 by Fred Meyer

Recipes by Leigh Ann Hieronymus

ISBN 978-0-9897104-2-8

Library of Congress Cataloging-in-Publication Data available.

Published by:

Fred Meyer

3800 SE 22ND Avenue
Portland, Oregon 97202-2918
www.fredmeyer.com

Developed and produced by Carpe Diem Books®

Carpe Diem Books®
Publisher: Ross Eberman
www.carpediembooks.com

Project Director: Richard Owsiany
Editorial Director / Marketing: Greg Mowery
Editor: Katherine Miller
Designer: William Campbell
Cover Photography: Christi Carlo, Iridio Studios
Food Stylist: Margaret Freeman
Food Photography: Carla Nalley
Indexer: Cher Paul
Prepress & Color Management: Mars Premedia
Printing & Binding: Multicolor Media Production Limited
Sales: Ken Rowe

First Edition

Manufactured in China
First Printing 2014

10 9 8 7 6 5 4 3 2 1

For my husband, Lefteris, my official taste-tester for this book and every meal at home. When he says to me in his native Greek, "για σου τα χέρια σας" (which roughly translates to bless your hands that made this…), it reminds me that I'm also in good hands.

Contents

Introduction

I CAN'T REMEMBER A TIME WHEN FOOD didn't play an important part of my life. As a young girl growing up in Columbus, Ohio, my dad loved to order such wonderful and unusual things as ash-rolled goat cheeses, bosc pears, and crates of artichokes as well as fine wines. At that time, these foods were very exotic. During summers in my teens I pedaled my bike to a small roadside fruit stand where I earned pocket money selling beautiful local produce. In my early twenties, I spent a nearly a year in Greece on my own. The memorable foods and stunning produce of the Mediterranean stayed with me throughout my life. Food has continued to play a big part in my career as well as my marriage.

Fourteen years ago, I came to work at Fred Meyer in Portland, Oregon. I've been an eyewitness to the huge growth of the food culture here in the Pacific Northwest. Creating recipes for TV and Fred Meyer has become an exciting part of what I do here. My goal is to help our customers prepare new and delicious meals with the foods they purchase in our stores. We're deeply involved in creating a satisfying shopping experience for our customers with local and organic produce, fresh seafood and meats, wines and beer, artisanal cheese, and much more. Initially I developed the in-store cooking program, "Cook and Tell." Then came *Fresh Ideas with Leigh Ann*, a television segment that has aired on *Oprah*, *Ellen*, the *Today* show, and other programs. During these segments—many of which can be accessed on the Fred Meyer website—I have an amazing opportunity to share a wide range of dishes, menus and techniques as well as timesaving tips.

I have created nearly 1,000 recipes for Fresh Ideas with Leigh Ann, so narrowing the choices for this cookbook has been a challenge. But the recipes you see here are 150 of my favorites, the dishes that I've cooked often for family and friends. After a long day at work, I'm faced with the same question as everyone else: "What's for dinner?" I rarely have time to spend an afternoon in the kitchen—most of us don't. A meal in my home has to come together quickly, using ingredients that are easy to find, taste great and, above all, be fresh.

As you explore my favorite recipes, I hope you'll have more time to enjoy great food surrounded by your family and friends.

Sweet and Savory Spiced Nuts, page 8

Twisted Parmesan Breadsticks, page 12

Gorgonzola-Pistachio Grapes, page 16

Fresh Parsley Dip, page 17

Appetizers

Grilled Mini Sweet Peppers

Sweet mini peppers are perfect for the grill. When I'm in a hurry, I grill them without coring and seeding. If you have any left over, they're great sliced and added to salads, a cheese board, or as a topping for sausages.

Makes 4 servings

---

2 pounds mini sweet peppers, cored and seeded through the tops but left whole

Wooden skewers

Olive oil, for brushing peppers

Salt and freshly ground black pepper

1. Preheat grill to medium heat. Meanwhile, soak skewers in water for 30 minutes.

2. Thread a soaked skewer through each pepper. Lightly brush with olive oil.

3. Grill for about 3 minutes per side. Season to taste with salt and pepper.

Tzatziki

My friends request this recipe more than any other.
It's a staple in my home as a dip for toasted pita chips
or freshly cut vegetables, and as a sauce for fish.

Makes 4 servings

4 cups plain whole-milk yogurt

1 large English cucumber, unpeeled, seeded
 and coarsely grated

2 cloves garlic, crushed

1 teaspoon salt

¼ teaspoon freshly ground black pepper

6 tablespoons chopped fresh dill

1. Line a large bowl with one layer of cheesecloth. Add yogurt and gather edges of cheesecloth together to form a ball. Tie the ends to a wooden spoon and suspend the ball over the bowl for 3 to 4 hours, until most of the water has drained.

2. Squeeze excess liquid out of the grated cucumber and add to a medium bowl. Add strained yogurt and stir well. Mix in the garlic, salt, pepper, and dill.

Sweet and Savory Spiced Nuts

Mom used to make these nuts when we had dinner guests coming over. If you're expecting a crowd, you can double the batch and store them for several weeks.

Makes 6 cups

6 cups unsalted mixed nuts, such as pecans, cashews, walnuts, and almonds

½ teaspoon ground coriander

½ teaspoon ground cumin

3 tablespoons butter

2 tablespoons firmly packed brown sugar

½ teaspoon Worcestershire sauce

½ teaspoon cayenne pepper

1 teaspoon salt

1. Preheat oven to 325°F.

2. Place nuts on a rimmed baking sheet. Bake until toasted, shaking the sheet several times during baking, about 10 to 15 minutes.

3. Meanwhile, in a small skillet over low heat, add coriander, cumin, butter, brown sugar, Worcestershire sauce, cayenne, and salt. Stir until the butter melts and sugar is dissolved.

4. Place nuts in a bowl, pour the warm spiced butter over the nuts; stir until well coated. Let the nuts cool completely and store in an airtight container.

Chickpea and Kalamata Olive Spread

I like to make variations of hummus. This one is
particularly nice on sandwiches, and perfect as a dip.

Makes 4 servings

1 (15.5-ounce) can chickpeas (garbanzo beans),
    drained and rinsed (1¾ cups)

⅓ cup kalamata olives, pitted

2 green onions, thinly sliced

1 tablespoon fresh lemon juice

Salt

Pinch cayenne pepper

⅓ cup olive oil

1. In a food processor, combine chickpeas, olives,
green onions, lemon juice, ¼ teaspoon salt, and
the cayenne; pulse to combine.

2. With the motor running, slowly add the olive
oil; process until smooth. Season to taste with
additional salt.

Smoked Salmon Puffs with Crème Fraîche

If you want to serve a special appetizer, this one is truly elegant—and it's fun and easy to make.

Makes 6 to 8 servings

1 sheet frozen puff pastry, thawed according to package directions

1 cup coarsely grated Kerrygold Dubliner or gruyère cheese

Freshly ground black pepper

¼ cup crème fraîche

1 (4-ounce) package thinly smoked salmon (lox variety)

Tiny sprigs fresh dill, for garnish

1. Preheat oven to 400°F. Line two baking sheets with parchment paper.

2. Roll puff pastry into a 14-inch square on a lightly floured board. Sprinkle evenly with cheese and pepper; cover with waxed paper. Using a rolling pin, press cheese and pepper firmly into dough; remove waxed paper. Cut dough into 6 strips vertically and 5 equal strips horizontally to make 30 pieces. Place on prepared baking sheets. Bake 8 to 10 minutes or until golden. Cool completely. (May be prepared a day ahead and stored in an airtight container.)

3. Spread a dab of crème fraîche on each puff. Top each with a small piece of folded salmon and dill sprig.

Twisted Parmesan Breadsticks

These are an alternative to everyday crackers. Serve them in a tall glass or basket on the dinner table, or with appetizers and wine.

Makes 2 dozen

1 (17.3-ounce) package frozen puff pastry, thawed according to package directions
Finely grated parmesan cheese
Salt and freshly ground black pepper

1. Preheat oven to 400°F. Line two baking sheets with parchment paper.

2. Roll out one sheet of puff pastry to smooth and flatten. Sprinkle to taste with cheese, salt, and pepper.

3. Slice into 1-inch-wide strips, twist, and place on prepared baking sheet. Repeat with second sheet of pastry.

4. Bake for 15 minutes, or until lightly browned. Cool and store in an airtight container.

Blue Cheese Mousse

This is lovely served with a sliced baguette, but for a special occasion try serving the mousse on baguette slices and topping with your favorite fruit or nuts. To ensure delicious results be sure to use a quality blue cheese—not the pre-crumbled variety.

Makes 4 servings

6 ounces blue cheese, crumbled (¾ cup)

1 (8-ounce) package neufchâtel or reduced-fat
    cream cheese, softened

½ cup heavy whipping cream

Salt and freshly ground black pepper

Baguette slices, crackers, or fruit, for serving

1. In a food processor, blend blue cheese and cream cheese until smooth. While machine is running, add cream in a slow, steady stream. Season to taste with salt and pepper. Refrigerate for 1 hour. Serve with baguette slices, crackers, or fruit.

Herbed Mushrooms in Crispy Phyllo

This elegant appetizer also works as a side dish—hot or cold—and turns even the most basic meal into something fancy.

Makes 4 servings

4 sheets frozen phyllo dough, thawed according to
    package directions

¼ cup butter, melted

2 tablespoons olive oil

1 clove garlic, crushed

4 cups sliced fresh shiitake or cremini mushrooms, or
    a mixture

1 tablespoon fresh thyme, chopped, plus 4 sprigs for
    garnish

Pinch salt

½ teaspoon freshly ground black pepper

2 tablespoons dry sherry

1. Preheat oven to 400°F.

2. Brush a standard muffin tin and sheets of phyllo pastry lightly with melted butter. Crumple each sheet loosely into a 4-inch circle. Gently press each round into a muffin tin cup. Bake the pastry for about 8 minutes, or until crisp.

3. Meanwhile, in a medium skillet, heat the olive oil over medium heat. Add the garlic, mushrooms, thyme, salt, pepper, and sherry; sauté for 6 to 8 minutes.

4. Spoon mushroom mixture into baked phyllo cups. Garnish each with a sprig of thyme.

Gorgonzola-Pistachio Grapes

These look like elegant little cheeseballs, but inside there's a fruity surprise. Warning: they can be addictive!

¾ cup shelled unsalted pistachios

4 ounces neufchâtel or reduced-fat cream cheese, softened

2 ounces gorgonzola cheese, crumbled (½ cup)

¼ cup heavy whipping cream

8 ounces red or green grapes

1. In a food processor, pulse the pistachios until coarsely chopped. Transfer to a bowl.

2. In another bowl, add cream cheese, gorgonzola, and cream; mix until well blended. Gently fold the grapes into the mixture until all are well coated.

3. Using a toothpick, remove a grape from the cheese mixture and roll in the chopped pistachios. Place on waxed paper and repeat with remaining grapes. Refrigerate in an air-tight container until ready to serve.

Fresh Parsley Dip

In Greek, this dip is called maidanosalata. It's a wonderful alternative to hummus or Tzatziki, and a good reason why no one should ever buy a commercial dip. Keep it in the refrigerator for a quick snack.

Makes 8 servings

6 slices sourdough bread

1½ bunches fresh Italian (flat-leaf) parsley, including
    stalks, roughly chopped

1 medium onion, roughly chopped

⅔ cup olive oil

¼ cup red wine vinegar

Salt and freshly ground black pepper

1. In a medium bowl, soak the bread in water for 10 to 15 minutes, then squeeze out all the excess moisture.

2. In a food processor, add the bread, parsley, and onion. Blend until smooth, slowly adding the oil and vinegar while the machine is running. Season to taste with salt and pepper. If the mixture seems too dry, add a little more oil and vinegar. Cover and refrigerate until ready to serve.

Meatballs and Spiced Yogurt Sauce

Lemongrass, ginger, and garlic flavor these fragrant meatballs.
I like to use lamb, but ground beef also works well. The tangy
yogurt sauce is a perfect foil for the rich meat.

Makes 4 to 6 servings

2 pounds ground lamb or beef

1 onion, minced

4 cloves garlic, minced, divided

2 tablespoons soy sauce

2 eggs, beaten

1 teaspoon peeled and finely grated fresh ginger

1 teaspoon finely grated lemongrass

2 tablespoons chopped fresh Italian (flat-leaf) parsley

Salt and freshly ground black pepper

3 cups plain Greek yogurt (low-fat or full-fat)

1 tablespoon fresh lemon juice

1 tablespoon olive oil

2 teaspoons ground cumin

1 teaspoon curry powder

¼ teaspoon cayenne pepper

1. Preheat oven to broil. Lightly grease a baking sheet.

2. In a large bowl, mix together ground beef, onion, 2 cloves minced garlic, soy sauce, eggs, ginger, lemongrass, parsley, ½ teaspoon salt, and ½ teaspoon pepper. Use mixture to roll 2-inch balls (about 24) and place 1½ inches apart on the prepared baking sheet. Broil 6 to 8 minutes, turning once.

3. Meanwhile, in a medium bowl, mix yogurt, remaining 2 cloves minced garlic, lemon juice, olive oil, cumin, curry powder, and cayenne. Season to taste with salt and pepper. Serve meatballs with yogurt sauce on the side.

Artichoke-Feta Bisque, page 25

Chilled Cantaloupe Soup, page 28

Fragrant Thai Coconut Soup, page 32

Fresh Asparagus Soup, page 33

Soups

Coconut-Lentil Soup

I've eaten a lot of lentil soup in my life and, because I love the flavor of coconut, I knew they would be great together.

2 cups dried lentils

4 cups vegetable or chicken broth

2 tablespoons olive oil

2 (14.5-ounce) cans diced tomatoes, undrained

3 carrots, peeled and diced

1 onion, chopped

1 cup chopped celery

2 cloves garlic, minced

½ teaspoon chili powder

¼ teaspoon cayenne pepper

1 teaspoon ground cumin

1 teaspoon sugar

1 teaspoon salt

½ cup water

2 (14-ounce) cans light coconut milk

1 tablespoon peeled and finely grated fresh ginger

2 tablespoons finely grated lemongrass

½ cup chopped fresh cilantro

1 lime, cut into wedges, for serving

1. Rinse the lentils and discard any that are discolored and any stones.

2. In a stockpot, combine the lentils, broth, oil, tomatoes, carrots, onion, celery, garlic, chili powder, cayenne, cumin, sugar, salt, and ½ cup water. Bring to a boil and reduce the heat to low. Cover the pan and simmer, stirring frequently, for 20 to 25 minutes, or until the lentils are just tender.

3. Stir in the coconut milk, ginger, and lemongrass; cook until heated through.

4. Garnish with cilantro and serve with a wedge of lime.

Velvet Egg Soup

I love this soup. It's quick to make in a pinch, and it's comforting for someone who's feeling under the weather.

Makes 4 servings

6 cups chicken broth

½ teaspoon reduced-sodium soy sauce

1 tablespoon cornstarch

3 large eggs, slightly beaten

½ teaspoon dark sesame oil

2 green onions, thinly sliced, for serving

1. In a stockpot, bring the chicken broth to a boil over high heat.

2. In a small bowl, combine soy sauce, cornstarch, and a tablespoon of the hot broth, mixing until smooth. Add to the chicken broth mixture and heat until slightly thickened.

3. Remove soup from the heat and slowly swirl in the beaten eggs so that the cooked egg forms strands.

4. To serve, stir in sesame oil and top with sliced green onions.

Artichoke-Feta Bisque

This is an uncommon but brilliant flavor combination for a soup. Feta cheese adds a salty, sharp note that compliments the artichoke, and the bisque makes an elegant starter course. The recipe is a snap to make, and you can even prepare it through step 2 up to a day ahead and refrigerate it. Be sure to use a feta made with goat's milk.

Makes 4 servings

1 tablespoon butter

1 onion, chopped

2 cups frozen artichokes hearts, thawed

4 cups chicken broth

¼ teaspoon dried thyme

¼ cup heavy whipping cream

1½ ounces feta cheese, crumbled (⅓ cup)

Salt and freshly ground black pepper

Fresh chives, snipped, for garnish

1. In a stockpot, melt butter over medium heat. Add onion and sauté about 5 minutes. Add artichokes, broth, and thyme. Simmer for 5 minutes; remove from heat and cool slightly.

2. Working in batches, purée artichoke mixture in blender or food processor until smooth.

3. Return puréed mixture to stockpot. Stir in cream and feta cheese. Simmer over medium heat, whisking constantly, until cheese melts, about 2 minutes.

4. Season to taste with salt and pepper. Serve garnished with snipped chives.

Sherried Zucchini Bisque

I just love zucchini, so I use it to make a hearty yet elegant soup. It's rich and luxurious.

2 tablespoons butter
1 medium onion, chopped
1 clove garlic, crushed
2 cups peeled and cubed potatoes
1 pound zucchini, coarsely grated, divided
2 cups chicken broth

1 medium carrot, peeled and coarsely grated
¼ cup dry sherry
3 tablespoons chopped fresh dill, plus sprigs for
    garnish
⅛ teaspoon ground nutmeg
½ teaspoon salt
½ teaspoon freshly ground black pepper
1 cup heavy whipping cream

1. In a stockpot, heat butter over medium heat; add onion and garlic and sauté for 2 minutes. Add potatoes, cover, and cook for 8 minutes, stirring often.

2. Reserve ½ cup zucchini for later; add remaining to potato mixture. Cook, covered, for 5 minutes, or until vegetables are tender. Working in batches, purée in a blender or food processor until mixture is smooth and return to stockpot.

3. Stir chicken broth into zucchini purée. Add carrot, sherry, chopped dill, nutmeg, salt, pepper, and reserved zucchini. Cook another 6 minutes. Stir in cream and heat until warmed through.

4. Serve garnished with dill sprigs.

Creamy Corn Chowder

My husband loves this creamy soup. Come summer, try making it with grilled corn sliced off the cob.

1 tablespoon butter

¼ cup chopped celery

¼ cup chopped onion

¼ cup cored and chopped red bell pepper

2 cups corn kernels, preferably from fresh or grilled
    corn

1 cup peeled and diced (½-inch) potato

1 cup vegetable or chicken broth

¼ teaspoon paprika

½ teaspoon salt

Freshly ground black pepper

2½ cups milk, divided

1½ tablespoons cornstarch

1. In a large saucepan, melt butter over medium heat. Add celery, onion, bell pepper, and corn; sauté for 2 minutes.

2. Add potato, broth, paprika, salt, and pepper to taste. Bring to a simmer, cover, and cook for 10 minutes, or until potato is tender.

3. Mix ½ cup milk with cornstarch. Slowly stir into hot soup. Add remaining 2 cups milk and heat until thickened.

Chilled Cantaloupe Soup

On a warm summer evening there's nothing more refreshing than a chilled fruit soup. Note that you need to make it at least an hour ahead to give the soup time to chill.

1 cantaloupe, peeled, seeded, and diced

2 cups fresh orange juice, divided

1 tablespoon fresh lime juice

1 pinch ground cinnamon

Fresh mint leaves, for garnish

1. In a blender or food processor, add cantaloupe and ½ cup orange juice; pulse until smooth. Transfer to large bowl.

2. Stir in lime juice, cinnamon, and remaining 1½ cups orange juice. Cover and refrigerate for at least 1 hour. Serve garnished with mint leaves.

Tomato-Rice Soup

Warm up with a steaming bowl of rich, homemade tomato soup. Fresh basil and parmesan balance the tomatoes (make sure they're ripe), and rice makes it a meal.

6 to 8 servings

3 medium tomatoes, diced

1 (46-ounce) bottle tomato juice

3 cups cooked brown rice

3 cups milk

1 teaspoon sugar

½ teaspoon salt

½ teaspoon freshly ground black pepper

½ cup shaved parmesan cheese

1 tablespoon shredded fresh basil

1. In a stockpot, combine the tomatoes, tomato juice, rice, milk, sugar, salt, and pepper; bring to a simmer over medium heat; stir and simmer about 10 minutes.

2. Serve garnished with cheese and basil.

Slow-Cooker Pork Posole

This savory stew is a favorite of my husband's. Think of it as a warming, wintery one-dish meal. If you find a pork butt roast that has a bone, just cook it with the bone and remove after it's tender.

Makes 6 servings

1 onion, diced

2 pounds boneless pork butt roast

2 (15-ounce) cans green enchilada sauce

1 (15-ounce) can hominy, drained

1 (7-ounce) can diced fire-roasted green chilies

4 cloves garlic, minced

Dash cayenne pepper

1 teaspoon ground cumin

½ teaspoon sugar

½ cup chopped fresh cilantro, for garnish

1 lime, cut into wedges, for serving

1. In a slow-cooker, add the onion and pork. Cover and cook on high for 3 to 4 hours.

2. Remove pork from cooker and shred with two forks. Skim or drain fat from meat juices. Return shredded meat to cooker with the juices.

3. To the cooker, add the enchilada sauce, hominy, chilies, garlic, cayenne, cumin, and sugar. Cook for 1 to 1½ hours.

4. Top with cilantro and serve with a wedge of lime.

Fragrant Thai Coconut Soup

This is another of my go-to recipes. It's loaded with flavors of lemongrass, ginger, and lime. Sometimes I add fresh zucchini or cherry tomatoes during the last few minutes of cooking.

Makes 4 to 6 servings

1 tablespoon olive oil

1 onion, diced

1 large carrot, peeled and sliced

1 large yam, peeled and cubed

1 large potato, peeled and cubed

4 cups vegetable or chicken broth

1 red bell pepper, cored and diced

1 (14-ounce) can light coconut milk

1 tablespoon minced garlic

2 tablespoons peeled and finely grated fresh ginger

2 tablespoons finely grated lemongrass

1 lime, cut into wedges, for serving

1. In a stockpot, heat oil over medium heat. Add onion and sauté until translucent.

2. Add carrot, yam, potato, and broth; cook until vegetables are tender, about 20 minutes.

3. Add bell pepper, coconut milk, garlic, ginger, and lemongrass; cook just until bell pepper is tender-crisp. Serve with a wedge of lime.

Fresh Asparagus Soup

This recipe was my answer to a friend's request for a soup that reminded him of his mother's simple but elegant French cooking.

Makes 4 servings

1 tablespoon butter

3 tablespoons minced shallot

1 quart chicken broth (4 cups)

4 cups trimmed and sliced (1-inch) asparagus

½ cup heavy whipping cream

Salt

Pinch cayenne pepper

1. In a stockpot, melt the butter over medium heat; add shallot and sauté for 1 minute.

2. Add broth and asparagus; simmer for 5 minutes, or until the asparagus is tender but still bright green.

3. Working in batches, ladle asparagus with a little broth into a blender or food processor and purée. Add purée back to pot. Repeat until all asparagus is puréed.

4. Stir cream into soup and simmer until heated through. Season to taste with salt and cayenne.

Lemon Tahini Soup

Tahini, a thick paste of ground sesame seeds, is often used as an ingredient in hummus. Few people think of it as something that could make a crazy delicious soup.

8 cups water

1 cup brown rice

Salt

2 lemons, juiced, divided

½ cup tahini

3 carrots, peeled and finely grated

3 green onions, chopped

¼ cup chopped fresh Italian (flat-leaf) parsley

Freshly ground black pepper

1. In a large pot, bring water to boil over high heat. Add rice and ½ teaspoon salt, bring to a simmer, reduce heat and cook until rice is tender, about 15 minutes.

2. Turn heat off and stir in half of the lemon juice.

3. In a medium bowl, add tahini and a ladleful of broth. Mix until smooth and add mixture back into pot.

4. Add carrots, green onions, parsley, and remaining lemon juice; simmer for 5 to 8 minutes. Season to taste with salt and pepper and serve.

Greek Beef Stew

If you find ordinary American beef stew stodgy, you'll love this flavorful Mediterranean version served with orzo pasta.

Makes 4 servings

¼ cup olive oil

2 pounds stew beef, cut into 1- to 2-inch chunks

1 medium onion, chopped

1 (14.5-ounce) can diced tomatoes, undrained

4 cloves garlic, minced

1 teaspoon dried oregano

2 tablespoons tomato paste

½ cup beef broth

Salt and freshly ground black pepper

1 pound orzo pasta, cooked according to package directions

⅓ cup grated kefalotiri or parmesan cheese, for serving (see note)

1. Preheat oven to 350°F.

2. In a large Dutch oven, heat the olive oil over high heat. Add beef and brown it, working in batches if necessary; transfer beef to a bowl.

3. To the Dutch oven, add the onion, tomatoes, garlic, and oregano; cook for 10 minutes, stirring occasionally.

4. Return beef to pan. Add the tomato paste and beef broth. Season to taste with salt and pepper.

5. Place lid on the pot and bake for 1½ to 2 hours, or until beef is tender.

6. Serve alongside hot orzo, and sprinkle with cheese.

Note: Kefalotiri cheese is a hard, salty goat and/or sheep's cheese from Greece. It is found at most cheese counters.

Salade Niçoise, page 42

Fresh Herb and Cherry Tomato Salad, page 46

Broccoli-Cauliflower Salad, page 47

Mukimame Salad with Cranberries & Hazelnuts, page 55

Salads

Grapes, Greens, and Feta Salad

The sweetness of grapes, and the saltiness of feta cheese play together beautifully in this salad. I like to use both red and green grapes for a vibrant presentation.

4 tablespoons olive oil, divided

2 tablespoons balsamic vinegar

1 teaspoon dried oregano

½ teaspoon salt

½ teaspoon freshly ground black pepper

6 cups mixed greens

8 ounces feta cheese, crumbled (2 cups)

1 pound red or green grapes, or a combination, halved

½ teaspoon minced fresh rosemary

¼ cup toasted and chopped slivered almonds

1. In a small bowl, whisk 3 tablespoons olive oil with the vinegar, oregano, salt, and pepper; set aside.

2. In a large bowl, add grapes, remaining 1 tablespoon oil, the rosemary, and feta. Toss gently and set aside.

3. In a separate bowl, toss greens with dressing. Place greens on serving plates. Top with feta/grape mixture, sprinkle with almonds, and serve.

Salade Niçoise

Salade Niçoise is a refreshing main dish salad that's perfect for warm weather. If you are in the mood to fire up the grill, sear fresh ahi tuna and serve it in this salad.

Makes 4 to 6 servings

2 cups diced (1-inch) red potatoes, unpeeled

2 cups green beans, trimmed

2 tablespoons Dijon mustard

2 tablespoons red wine vinegar

1 tablespoon mayonnaise (preferably a brand made with olive oil)

Salt and freshly ground black pepper

3 tablespoons olive oil

3 tablespoons chopped fresh herbs, such as tarragon, chives, basil, dill, or a combination

6 cups baby greens

2 (5-ounce) cans solid white albacore tuna, drained

1 cup peeled and shredded carrots

1 cup thinly sliced radishes

¾ cup niçoise or kalamata olives

4 large hard-cooked eggs, cut into wedges

1. Bring a pot of lightly salted water to a boil. Add potatoes and cook for 6 minutes, or until tender. Remove potatoes and set aside to cool (keep water on the boil). Add green beans to pot and cook for 3 minutes, or just until crisp-tender. Drain in a colander, rinse with cold water and pat dry.

2. In a medium bowl, whisk the mustard, vinegar, mayonnaise, and salt and pepper to taste. Slowly add the oil, whisking, until the dressing is emulsified. Stir in the herbs and set aside.

3. Place baby greens on serving plates. Arrange the green beans, potatoes, tuna, carrots, radishes, olives, and eggs on top. Drizzle with dressing and serve at room temperature or chilled.

Moroccan Turkey Salad

Serving roast turkey often means leftovers. By combining them in a salad with couscous, fresh oranges, and warm spices, you create an exotic one-dish meal.

Makes 2 to 3 servings

4 cups cooked couscous, cooled

3 tablespoons dried currants

¼ cup slivered almonds, toasted

¼ teaspoon ground cinnamon

1½ tablespoons chopped fresh mint

Salt and freshly ground black pepper

⅓ cup olive oil

1 tablespoon fresh lemon juice

1 tablespoon fresh orange juice

1 tablespoon chopped fresh cilantro

1 teaspoon honey

3 teaspoons ground cumin

2 cups cubed (1-inch) cooked turkey breast

1⅓ cups peeled and halved orange segments

1 cup cored, thinly sliced and separated fennel

1. In a large bowl, combine couscous, currants, almonds, cinnamon, mint, and salt and pepper to taste. Set aside.

2. In another large bowl, whisk together olive oil, lemon juice, orange juice, cilantro, honey, cumin, salt, and pepper to taste. Add turkey, orange segments, and fennel. Spoon turkey mixture on top of couscous and serve at room temperature.

Watermelon, Arugula, and Feta Salad with Pistachios

Sweet watermelon, bitter arugula, and salty feta make a brilliant combination. The salad works well as both side dish—try for grilled seafood—or as a meal on its own.

Makes 4 servings

1 tablespoon white balsamic vinegar

1 tablespoon fresh lemon juice

¼ teaspoon salt

2 tablespoons olive oil

3 cups cubed (¾-inch) watermelon

3 cups arugula

2 cups fresh baby spinach

1 cup coarsely chopped fresh mint

¼ cup shelled unsalted pistachios

Freshly ground black pepper

1½ ounces feta cheese, crumbled (⅓ cup)

1. In a large bowl, mix vinegar, lemon juice, and salt. Whisk in oil.

2. Add watermelon, arugula, spinach, mint, and pistachios; toss well. Season to taste with pepper, top with feta, and serve.

SALADS

Fresh Herb and Cherry Tomato Salad

Cherry and grape tomatoes are available year-round and make a wonderful salad on their own without greens. Here I've complemented their sweet flavor with shallot, and fresh basil and marjoram.

Makes 2 servings

1 small shallot, finely diced

1 tablespoon olive oil

2 teaspoons chopped fresh marjoram

2 tablespoons shredded fresh basil

Salt and freshly ground black pepper

3 cups mixed grape or cherry tomatoes, halved

White balsamic vinegar

1. In a medium bowl, mix shallot, olive oil, marjoram, basil, and salt and pepper to taste; drizzle over tomatoes. Sprinkle salad with vinegar to taste and serve.

Broccoli-Cauliflower Salad with Creamy Lemon Dressing

Broccoli and cauliflower are nutritional powerhouses and give this salad a wonderful crunchy texture. A touch of lemon juice gives a tangy note to the creamy dressing.

Makes 3 to 4 servings

1 cup sour cream

1 teaspoon dried oregano, crushed

1 teaspoon celery seeds

2 tablespoons fresh lemon juice

¼ cup finely chopped onion

½ teaspoon salt

½ teaspoon freshly ground black pepper

4 cups roughly chopped (1 inch) romaine lettuce

1 cup cored and roughly chopped (1 inch) red bell pepper

1 cup roughly chopped (1-inch) broccoli

1 cup roughly chopped (1-inch) cauliflower

1 cup roughly chopped (1-inch) mushrooms

1 cup thawed and roughly chopped (1-inch) artichoke hearts

6 kalamata olives, pitted and chopped

1. In a medium bowl, whisk sour cream, oregano, celery seeds, lemon juice, onion, salt, and pepper; set aside.

2. In a large bowl, toss lettuce, bell pepper, broccoli, cauliflower, mushrooms, artichoke hearts, and olives. Add dressing, toss gently, and serve.

Spicy Halloumi, Avocado, and Mango Salad

If you haven't tried halloumi, you're in for a treat. It's an unripened brined cheese that has a high melting point, so it can be fried or grilled. I toss it with creamy avocado, sweet mango, pomegranate, red pepper flakes, and cumin for a unique and delicious salad.

Makes 4 servings

2 tablespoons olive oil

1 teaspoon cumin seeds

1 teaspoon crushed red pepper flakes

½ cup cubed (1-inch) halloumi cheese

½ teaspoon ground cumin

2 tablespoons chopped fresh cilantro

1 tablespoon chopped fresh mint

Salt

2 medium avocados

½ lemon, juiced

2 mangoes, peeled, pitted and cubed (1-inch)

1 pomegranate, seeded, divided

2 cups baby greens

1. In a medium skillet, heat oil over medium heat. Add cumin seeds, pepper flakes, and cheese; sauté for 3 to 4 minutes, until browned. Remove skillet from heat and sprinkle on ground cumin, cilantro, mint, and salt to taste.

2. Meanwhile, halve, pit, and peel avocados. Cut into 1-inch cubes and toss with the lemon juice. Add to cooled cheese along with mango and half of the pomegranate seeds. Mix gently so that the spices coat the fruit.

3. Arrange greens on plates. Spoon the salad on top, sprinkle with the remaining pomegranate seeds, and serve.

Honey-Yogurt Waldorf Salad

Using yogurt in a Waldorf salad gives it a lighter, brighter flavor. Lemon and a touch of honey bring it all together.

Makes 4 servings

½ cup plain yogurt

2 tablespoons mayonnaise (preferably a brand made with olive oil)

1 teaspoon honey

½ lemon, juiced

½ teaspoon finely grated lemon zest

3 large apples, cored and diced

¾ cup chopped celery

¼ cup raisins

⅓ cup walnut halves, toasted

1. In a small bowl, whisk together the yogurt, mayonnaise, honey, lemon juice, and lemon zest.

2. In a large bowl, place apples, celery, and raisins. Add dressing and gently toss. Refrigerate until well chilled.

3. Just before serving, gently stir in walnuts.

Fresh Greens, Orange, and Prosciutto Salad

You may not have thought of using prosciutto in a salad, but here its salty, savory flavor really heightens the sweetness of the oranges.

Makes 4 servings

1 tablespoon honey

1 teaspoon spicy brown mustard

1 tablespoon red wine vinegar

1 teaspoon poppy seeds

3 tablespoons olive oil

1 navel orange, peeled, sections separated and
    halved

1 avocado, pitted, peeled and cubed (½-inch)

1 cup thinly sliced English cucumber

5 cups baby greens or baby endive

12 slices prosciutto, cut into 2-inch pieces

1. In a small bowl, mix honey, mustard, vinegar, and poppy seeds. Gradually whisk in oil, whisking until emulsified.

2. Divide greens among serving plates, then alternately top with orange, cucumber, and avocado. Top with prosciutto, drizzle with dressing, and serve.

51

Kale Caesar Salad

There's nothing unusual about Caesar salad—unless it's made with kale. Here the hearty green stands in for the typical romaine lettuce, with amazing results.

Caesar Salad Dressing:
¼ teaspoon salt

1 teaspoon freshly ground black pepper

4 cloves garlic, finely minced

2 anchovy fillets, rinsed and patted dry

2 teaspoons Dijon mustard

2 large egg yolks

2 tablespoons fresh lemon juice

½ cup olive oil

1 teaspoon Worcestershire sauce

Salad:
½ loaf day-old artisan bread, cut into 1-inch cubes

¼ cup olive oil

1 clove garlic, minced

1 teaspoon dried basil

1 teaspoon dried dill

1 teaspoon dried oregano

Salt and freshly ground black pepper

6 cups stemmed and thinly sliced (½-inch) fresh kale

½ cup Caesar Salad Dressing

½ lemon, juiced, plus wedges for serving

⅓ cup grated parmesan cheese

To make dressing:

1. In a large wooden bowl combine salt, pepper, and minced garlic. Work the mixture into a paste using the back of a spoon. Add anchovies, blending the same way, then the mustard, egg yolks, lemon juice, olive oil, and Worcestershire sauce. This can also be whipped up in a blender.

To make salad:

1. Preheat oven to 400°F.

2. In a large mixing bowl, add bread cubes. In a small bowl, mix oil, garlic, herbs, and salt and pepper to taste; toss with bread.

3. Arrange cubes on a baking sheet and bake until toasted, 5 to 8 minutes. Remove from oven and set aside to cool.

4. In a small bowl, thin Caesar dressing with juice from half of the lemon. Toss shredded kale with dressing. Add croutons and toss. Garnish with parmesan and serve with lemon wedges alongside.

Blue Cheese Steak Salad with Sour Cream-Buttermilk Dressing

There's something about a steak salad that's really satisfying. My version adds several layers of flavors with tangy buttermilk, bitter arugula and briny kalamata olives.

Makes 4 servings

1 tablespoon olive oil

2 pounds New York strip steak

Salt and freshly ground black pepper

¼ cup sour cream

¼ cup buttermilk

1 teaspoon red wine vinegar

3 green onions, chopped

3 ounces blue cheese, crumbled (¾ cup)

4 cups chopped (2-inch) romaine lettuce

4 cups arugula

2 cups halved cherry tomatoes

¼ cup kalamata olives, pitted

1. In a large skillet, heat oil over medium-high heat. Season the steak on both sides with salt and pepper; add to skillet and cook 4 to 5 minutes per side (medium-rare). Transfer steaks to a cutting board, tent loosely with foil, and let rest 5 minutes. Cut into bite-size pieces.

2. In a small bowl, mix together sour cream, buttermilk, vinegar, green onions and ¼ teaspoon each salt and pepper. Stir in blue cheese.

3. In a large bowl, combine lettuce, arugula, and tomatoes. Toss with dressing. Divide salad among serving plates, top with steak and olives, and serve.

Mukimame Salad with Cranberries and Hazelnuts

Mukimame is the Japanese name for shelled fresh soy beans. They're sold in the frozen foods aisle and are so easy to prepare. Toss them with feta, dried cranberries, toasted hazelnuts, and a simple oil-and-vinegar dressing and you have a special salad.

Makes 2 to 3 servings

1 (10-ounce) bag frozen mukimame, prepared
    according to package directions
½ cup dried cranberries
1½ ounces feta cheese, crumbled (⅓ cup)
2 tablespoons olive oil
1 teaspoon rice wine vinegar
3 green onions, chopped
Salt and freshly ground black pepper
⅓ cup chopped toasted hazelnuts

1. In a large bowl, combine mukimame, cranberries, feta, oil, vinegar, green onions, and salt and pepper to taste; toss and refrigerate. Just before serving, gently stir in hazelnuts.

Sea Scallops and Fettuccine with Fresh Herb Pesto, page 61

Orecchiette with Spinach, Walnuts & Blue Cheese, page 65

Tabouleh, page 68

Chanterelle and Cremini Mushroom Risotto, page 69

Pasta, Rice, and Grains

Shrimp Linguine with Fresh Tomatoes, Mushrooms, and Garlic

Although tomatoes are at their best in summer, this dish is terrific any time of year. It's packed with produce, and because the sauce is cooked ever so briefly, it really retains a fresh flavor.

1 pound dried linguine

2 tablespoons olive oil

1 pound large wild shrimp, peeled and deveined, with tails left on

3 cloves garlic, minced

1½ cups sliced fresh mushrooms

3½ cups fresh tomatoes, seeded and chopped

¾ cup chopped fresh basil

¼ cup chopped fresh Italian (flat-leaf) parsley, divided

½ teaspoon crushed red pepper flakes

Salt and freshly ground black pepper

1. Cook pasta in boiling salted water until al dente; drain and return to pot.

2. Meanwhile, in a large skillet, heat 1 tablespoon oil over medium-high heat. Add shrimp and garlic and sauté until cooked through, about 3 minutes. Remove shrimp from pan and cover.

3. Add remaining 1 tablespoon oil to same skillet and place over medium heat. Add mushrooms and sauté about 6 minutes. Add tomatoes, basil, 3 tablespoons parsley, and the red pepper flakes; cook for another 5 minutes.

4. Add mushroom-tomato mixture to pasta and toss. Season to taste with salt and pepper. Top with shrimp and remaining 1 tablespoon parsley and serve.

PASTA, RICE, AND GRAINS

59

Broccoli and Kalamata Olive Mostaccioli

This colorful pasta dish makes a festive side, or even a meatless main course. It's quick to make, and I also love that it's not smothered in a heavy cream sauce or lots of cheese.

Makes 6 to 8 servings

1 pound broccoli, divided into bite-sized florets

1 pound mostaccioli, penne or other tube-shaped pasta

2 tablespoons olive oil

1 large onion, finely chopped

1 clove garlic, crushed

1 (14.5-ounce) can crushed tomatoes, undrained

⅔ cup kalamata olives, pitted and sliced

2 tablespoons fresh thyme, chopped

¼ cup finely grated parmesan cheese

1. Bring a large pot of salted water to a boil. Add broccoli and cook just until tender-crisp; do not drain water. Use a slotted spoon to remove broccoli from pot and transfer to a bowl. Add pasta to boiling water and cook until al dente; drain, return to pot, and keep warm.

2. Meanwhile, in a large heavy skillet, heat the oil over medium heat. Add the onion and garlic, and sauté until soft, about 5 minutes. Add the tomatoes, olives, cooked broccoli, and thyme and cook for about 3 minutes.

3. Add the sauce to the pasta and toss gently. Add the parmesan, toss, and serve.

Sea Scallops and Fettuccine with Fresh Herb Pesto

Preparing a fresh herb pesto is a wonderful way to bring a bright flavor to pasta without overpowering the delicate scallops.

Makes 4 to 6 servings

¾ cup fresh basil

¾ cup fresh mint

⅓ cup fresh Italian (flat-leaf) parsley

¼ cup fresh sage

⅓ cup finely grated parmesan cheese

¼ cup chopped walnuts, lightly toasted

½ teaspoon salt

¼ teaspoon freshly ground black pepper

6 tablespoons olive oil

1 pound dried fettuccine

1 pound sea scallops

2 tablespoons chopped fresh dill, divided

1 tablespoon vegetable oil

1. In the bowl of a food processor fitted with metal blade, pulse together basil, mint, parsley, and sage. Add parmesan, walnuts, salt, and pepper; process to combine. With motor running, slowly add olive oil through the feed tube until mixture forms a paste.

2. Cook pasta in boiling salted water until al dente; drain and return to pot.

3. In a medium bowl, combine scallops and 1 tablespoon dill. In a large skillet, heat vegetable oil over medium-high heat. When oil is hot, add scallops; cook 2 minutes. Turn scallops and cook until they are just cooked through, 2 to 3 minutes more (be careful not to overcook them).

4. Stir pesto into hot pasta. Stir in scallops and remaining 1 tablespoon dill. Transfer to warm bowls and serve.

Pasta with Scallops and Tarragon

Wine and lime juice add bright acidity to this light and simple dish. The flavors of shallots and tarragon add a refined note to the succulent scallops.

Makes 4 to 6 servings

1 pound thin spaghetti

Salt and freshly ground black pepper

6 tablespoons butter, divided

1 clove garlic, minced

1 medium shallot, minced

1½ pounds bay scallops

¼ cup dry white wine

¼ cup fresh lime juice

2 tablespoons chopped fresh tarragon,
    plus more for garnish

1. Cook pasta in boiling salted water until al dente; drain and return to pot.

2. Meanwhile, pat scallops dry and season with salt and pepper. In a large skillet, heat 3 tablespoons butter over medium-high heat. When foam subsides, add garlic and shallots and sauté for 3 minutes. Add half of scallops, sauté until golden, about 3 minutes. Transfer with a slotted spoon to a bowl. Cook remaining scallops in remaining 3 tablespoons butter. Place all scallops in skillet and stir in wine, lime juice, and tarragon.

3. Toss pasta with scallops. Garnish with additional tarragon and serve.

PASTA, RICE, AND GRAINS

63

Linguine with Garlic, Olive Oil, and Red Pepper

This Italian favorite is great as a meal, or as a side dish for shrimp or chicken. Be sure to use a fruity, good quality olive oil.

Makes 4 servings

1 pound dried linguine

½ cup olive oil

2 cloves garlic

Salt

1 teaspoon crushed red pepper flakes

⅓ cup chopped fresh Italian (flat-leaf) parsley

Freshly ground black pepper

1. Cook pasta in boiling salted water until al dente; drain and return to pot.

2. Meanwhile, in a saucepan, heat the oil over medium heat; add garlic and a pinch of salt and cook gently, stirring, until the garlic is golden. Add red pepper flakes.

3. Toss the pasta with the oil. Add parsley and season to taste with pepper and additional salt. Toss well and serve.

Orecchiette with Spinach, Walnuts, and Blue Cheese

This quick dish is perfect for weeknight meals—especially when you use the convenient bags of washed baby spinach. The richness of the blue cheese and nuts is all it takes to create the simple, flavorful sauce.

Makes 4 servings

1 pound orecchiette pasta

3 tablespoons olive oil

3 cups baby spinach leaves

2 tablespoons rice vinegar

3 tablespoons chopped fresh chives

8 ounces blue cheese, crumbled (1 cup)

½ cup walnuts, toasted

Freshly ground black pepper

1. Cook pasta in boiling salted water until al dente; drain and return to pot.

2. In a large skillet, heat oil over medium-high heat. Add spinach and sauté for about 3 minutes. Add the vinegar.

3. To pasta, add spinach, chives, cheese, walnuts, and pepper to taste; toss well and serve.

Spaghetti with Creamy Cantaloupe Sauce

Growing up, one of my favorite Italian restaurants served this dish. Years later, I re-created it, and the results are amazing. Everyone I make it for falls in love with it.

12 ounces spaghetti

¼ cup butter

1 cantaloupe (the riper the better), peeled and cubed (2-inch)

1 tablespoon tomato paste

¼ teaspoon cayenne pepper

¾ teaspoon salt

½ cup half-and-half

Freshly ground black pepper

⅓ cup pumpkin seed kernels, toasted

1. Cook pasta in boiling salted water until al dente; drain and return to pot.

2. In a large skillet, heat butter over medium heat. Add melon and sauté until it breaks down. (It will still have lumps in it.)

3. Add tomato paste, cayenne, and salt; cook for 3 more minutes. Add half-and-half and black pepper to taste; remove from heat.

4. Toss sauce with spaghetti, top with pumpkin seeds, and serve.

PASTA, RICE, AND GRAINS

Tabouleh

Bulgur isn't a grain that's used often, but I love its chewy texture, especially when mixed with extra-fresh herbs. I always keep bulgur in my pantry so I can make Tabouleh when my neighbor brings me parsley fresh from her garden. And this salad is just as delicious served the next day.

Makes 3 to 4 servings

1 cup bulgur (cracked wheat)

1½ cups boiling water

¼ cup olive oil

3 tablespoons fresh lemon juice

1 clove garlic, minced

1½ teaspoons chopped fresh mint,
   plus extra leaves for garnish

½ teaspoon salt

½ cup chopped green onions

1½ cups chopped fresh Italian (flat-leaf) parsley

1 tomato, chopped

1. In large bowl, mix bulgur and boiling water; cover. Let stand 20 minutes or until bulgur is soft. If there is any unabsorbed water, drain it.

2. Stir in oil, lemon juice, garlic, mint, salt, green onions, parsley, and tomato; mix lightly. Garnish with mint leaves and serve.

Chanterelle and Cremini Mushroom Risotto

People don't make risotto often because they think it's difficult or tricky. But while it feels like a special occasion meal, it's a relatively simple dish to prepare. While you are stirring the rice and broth, you can enjoy talking with your guests. Please do buy arborio rice, a short-grain Italian variety that yields a creamy risotto and—provided you don't overcook it—nice chewy grains.

Makes 2 to 3 servings

1 tablespoon olive oil

1½ cups chopped onions

1 clove garlic, crushed

1 teaspoon chopped fresh Italian (flat-leaf) parsley

Salt and freshly ground black pepper

1 cup sliced fresh chanterelle mushrooms (or other variety of your choice)

1 cup sliced fresh cremini mushrooms

1 cup arborio rice

3 cups chicken or vegetable broth

½ cup 2-percent milk

¼ cup heavy whipping cream

3 tablespoons butter

1 cup finely grated parmesan cheese

1. In a large skillet, heat oil over medium heat. Add onion and garlic and sauté until onion is tender. Add parsley, ½ teaspoon salt, ½ teaspoon pepper, and mushrooms. Reduce heat to low and continue cooking until the mushrooms are soft.

2. Add the rice and stir for 2 minutes. Add 1 cup of broth, stirring until it has all been absorbed. Repeat with second cup of broth. Use just enough of the remaining cup of broth to cook rice until it is no longer chewy, but still firm and not mushy. You may not need all of the broth.

3. Add milk and cream, stirring until it is absorbed. Stir in the butter and cheese; remove from heat. Season to taste with additional salt and pepper; serve hot.

PASTA, RICE, AND GRAINS

Curried Brown Rice and Toasted Coconut Salad

This dish needs to be made ahead and chilled, which makes it convenient for entertaining. Preparing the rice with coconut milk adds a wonderful richness, which is further enhanced with peanut butter and lime juice.

Makes 4 to 6 servings

2 cups brown rice

1 (14-ounce) can light coconut milk

2¾ cups water

2 large limes, juiced

¼ cup creamy peanut butter

¼ cup dark sesame oil

1 teaspoon curry powder

1 clove garlic, crushed

Salt and freshly ground black pepper

¼ cup unsweetened dried coconut, toasted

½ cup raisins

¼ cup slivered almonds, toasted

1. In a saucepan, combine rice, coconut milk, and water. Bring to a boil, then cover and reduce heat to low. Simmer for 15 to 20 minutes, or until the rice has absorbed all of the liquid. Set aside to cool, with the lid on.

2. In a small bowl, stir together lime juice, peanut butter, sesame oil, curry powder, and garlic. Season to taste with salt and pepper.

3. When the rice has cooled, stir in dressing, coconut, and raisins. Refrigerate for 1 hour. Add almonds just before serving.

Wild Rice Pilaf with Citrus and Dried Fruit

Wild rice has a nutty flavor and a hearty texture that doesn't turn mushy. Although wild rice takes a bit longer to cook than white rice, it's well-worth the time. The dried fruit turns it into a robust side dish, which can become a one-dish meal just by adding chicken or shrimp.

Makes 4 servings

3 cups vegetable or chicken broth

1½ cups wild rice

1 tablespoon butter

1 onion, chopped

2 teaspoons firmly packed brown sugar

¼ cup golden raisins

¼ cup dried cranberries or dried cherries

¼ cup chopped dried apricots

1 tablespoon finely grated orange zest

1 orange, juiced

½ teaspoon freshly ground black pepper

2 tablespoons chopped fresh Italian (flat-leaf) parsley

1. In a medium saucepan, combine broth and rice; bring to boil, reduce heat, cover, and simmer 40 minutes or until rice is almost tender.

2. In small saucepan, melt butter over low heat. Stir in onion and brown sugar and cook 10 minutes, stirring occasionally, until onion is tender and lightly browned.

3. To the rice, add the cooked onions, raisins, cranberries, apricots, orange zest, orange juice, and pepper. Cover and simmer 10 minutes or until rice is tender and grains have puffed open.

4. Stir in parsley and serve warm.

Lemony Corn and Quinoa Salad

Quinoa is a wonderful grain that's packed with protein. Toss in some fresh mint and lemon zest and you get a burst of vivid flavors.

Makes 4 servings

3 cups fresh or frozen corn kernels

1 cup thinly sliced green onions

¾ cup chopped fresh mint

1 teaspoon finely grated lemon zest

¼ cup fresh lemon juice

¼ cup olive oil

2 cups cooked quinoa

Salt and freshly ground black pepper

1. Bring a pot of water to a boil. Add corn and cook for 2 minutes. Drain and let cool slightly.

2. In a large bowl, mix corn, green onions, mint, lemon zest, lemon juice, and oil. Add quinoa and mix well. Season to taste with salt and pepper. Serve at room temperature or chilled.

PASTA, RICE, AND GRAINS

Dijon-Brown Sugar Cedar Plank Salmon, page 79

Classic Crab Louis, page 89

Clams Steamed in Wine, Garlic, and Oregano, page 90

Coconut-Lemongrass-Lime Shrimp, page 91

Seafood

Mandarin Steelhead in Parchment

This steelhead is moist, with a delicate balance of sweet citrus and briny olives. The parchment paper makes for an elegant presentation, too.

Makes 4 servings

¼ cup pitted and sliced green olives

1 red bell pepper, thinly sliced

1 teaspoon chopped fresh oregano

3 mandarin oranges, one zested, all peeled and segmented

6 green onions (including tops), chopped, divided

2 lemons, juiced

4 (8-by-12-inch) sheets parchment paper

4 (6-ounce) steelhead fillets

½ teaspoon salt

½ teaspoon freshly ground black pepper

1. Preheat oven to 400°F. Place two baking sheets in oven.

2. In a medium bowl, combine olives, red bell pepper, oregano, mandarin zest and segments, half of the green onions, and lemon juice; set aside.

3. Lay out parchment paper. Divide remaining green onions evenly on one half of each parchment sheet. Place a steelhead fillet on each bed of green onions; sprinkle with salt and pepper. Top with orange mixture. Fold sheets of parchment over the top of fish and crimp the edges together, making small overlapping folds along the edge to seal tightly.

4. Place packets on heated baking sheets and bake 15 to 18 minutes. Transfer packets to individual plates. To serve, make a slice in the middle of each packet and tear the paper open to reveal the fish. Be very careful to avoid the hot steam.

SEAFOOD

Salmon with Tarragon-Basil Herb Oil

Salmon doesn't need a fancy preparation. Drizzling grilled fillets with a fresh herb-infused olive oil is all it takes to make a fragrant and winning meal.

Makes 4 servings

4 (6- to 8-ounce) wild salmon fillets

¼ cup olive oil, plus additional for brushing fish

1 tablespoon finely chopped fresh tarragon

1 tablespoon finely chopped fresh basil

1 tablespoon finely chopped fresh mint

Salt and freshly ground black pepper

1 lemon, cut into wedges, for serving

1. Preheat grill to medium. Lightly brush salmon with oil on both sides. Place on grill, skin side up, close lid and cook for 3 to 4 minutes. Carefully flip fish and grill for another 2 to 3 minutes, until an instant-read thermometer inserted in thickest part of fish measures 145°F. Remove fish from grill and tent loosely with foil.

2. Heat remaining ¼ cup oil in a small pan on grill. Add tarragon, basil, mint, and salt and pepper to taste. Heat for 30 seconds. Drizzle salmon with herb oil and serve with lemon wedges.

Dijon-Brown Sugar Cedar Plank Salmon

Grilling on cedar imparts a subtle but amazing flavor to salmon—which is probably why this is a Northwest favorite. I make this dish all summer long, even on weeknights.

Makes 4 to 6 servings

1 cedar plank (untreated, culinary grade)

Salt and freshly ground black pepper

¼ cup Dijon mustard

6 tablespoons firmly packed brown sugar

2 pounds wild salmon fillets

1 lemon, cut into wedges, for serving

1. Soak cedar plank in water for 30 minutes.

2. Preheat grill to medium heat. Lightly season the salmon with salt and pepper and place on soaked plank. Spread mustard to completely cover fish. Sprinkle the brown sugar over the mustard.

3. Place the plank in the center of the grill, close lid, and cook 15 to 20 minutes, or until an instant-read thermometer inserted in thickest part of fish measures 145°F. Keep a squirt bottle of water nearby to extinguish any flames on the plank. Serve with a squeeze of fresh lemon.

SEAFOOD

Dilled Salmon Croquettes

My grandmother used to make this recipe, but it's definitely worthy of an encore. The croquettes look like little hay stacks, and you'll love the creamy white sauce.

Makes 4 servings

1 (14.75-ounce) can salmon

1 teaspoon dried dill

1 teaspoon chopped capers

1 cup crushed saltine crackers

1 medium onion, finely chopped

1 large egg, slightly beaten

1 tablespoon olive oil

2 tablespoons cornstarch

1¼ cups milk (not skim)

¼ teaspoon salt

¼ teaspoon freshly ground white pepper

2 tablespoons butter

1 cup petite peas

1 lemon, cut into wedges, for serving

1. In a large bowl, mix salmon, dill, capers, cracker crumbs, onion, and egg. Shape into croquettes, like little haystacks, and place on a large plate or platter. Refrigerate for 20 minutes.

2. Preheat oven to 425 degrees. Oil a large baking sheet. Transfer croquettes to preparing baking sheet and bake for 15 to 20 minutes.

3. Meanwhile, in a small pan, whisk together cornstarch and milk over medium heat. Add salt, pepper, and butter; bring to a boil, stirring constantly. When mixture thickens, stir in peas.

4. Squeeze lemon wedges over the croquettes, top with sauce, and serve.

Crab, Asparagus, and Avocado Salad

I keep this crab salad light and bright tasting by using Greek yogurt. This is also a great dish for entertaining because it can be made ahead and chilled.

Makes 4 servings

8 ounces asparagus

1 cup plain Greek yogurt (low-fat or full-fat)

¼ cup mayonnaise (preferably a brand made with olive oil)

1 teaspoon white Worcestershire sauce

1 teaspoon Dijon mustard

1 dash hot pepper sauce

1 teaspoon capers, chopped

2 tablespoons chopped fresh Italian (flat-leaf) parsley

1 avocado, pitted, peeled, and sliced

Fresh lemon juice

¼ cup pitted and chopped kalamata olives

1 pound shelled crabmeat

1 cup frozen artichokes hearts, thawed and chopped

Freshly ground black pepper

Lettuce leaves or fresh tomato slices, for serving

1. Trim tough ends from asparagus and cut into 2-inch lengths. Steam just until tender-crisp and immediately rinse in cold water to stop cooking; set aside.

2. In a medium bowl, stir together yogurt, mayonnaise, white Worcestershire sauce, mustard, hot sauce, capers, and parsley; set aside.

3. In a large bowl, add avocado slices and squeeze a little lemon juice over them. Add asparagus, olives, crabmeat, and artichoke. Pour sauce over salad and gently mix. Season to taste with black pepper.

4. Serve salad on lettuce or with sliced tomatoes.

Mediterranean Baked Cod

True cod, aka Pacific cod, is mild, clean tasting, and a sustainable seafood choice. Here I've given it an Italian flavor with oregano, tomatoes, and garlic. The vegetables help keep the fish moist, while the panko topping cooks up light and crispy.

Makes 4 servings

1½ to 2 pounds true cod fillets

Salt and freshly ground black pepper

2 lemons, juiced

1 (14.5-ounce) can diced tomatoes, undrained

2 teaspoons dried oregano, crushed

3 cloves garlic, minced

2 tablespoons chopped fresh Italian (flat-leaf) parsley

½ cup panko bread crumbs

1½ teaspoons olive oil

1. Preheat oven to 375°F.

2. Place fish in a baking dish and season with salt, pepper, and lemon juice.

3. In a medium bowl, combine tomatoes, oregano, garlic, and parsley; pour over fish.

4. In a medium bowl, toss panko crumbs with oil and sprinkle over fish.

5. Bake until fish is just opaque inside, about 10 minutes per inch of thickness, or until an instant-read thermometer inserted in thickest part of fish measures 145°F. Serve.

Crispy Beer-Battered Halibut

These bite-size nuggets of halibut are perfect for game day, or anytime. To ensure that your nuggets are succulent, be sure not to overcook them. And don't forget the tartar sauce!

Makes 2 to 3 servings

Vegetable oil, for frying

2 cloves garlic, minced

2 tablespoons chopped fresh Italian (flat-leaf) parsley

1 teaspoon paprika

½ teaspoon cayenne pepper

½ teaspoon salt

½ teaspoon freshly ground black pepper

2 large eggs, beaten

1 (12-ounce) bottle pale beer

2 cups all-purpose flour

1 pound halibut fillets, skin removed, cut into 2-inch
  chunks

Tartar sauce, for serving

1. Heat 2 to 3 inches oil in fryer or deep skillet to 350°F.

2. In a large bowl, combine garlic, parsley, paprika, cayenne, salt, pepper, and eggs. Add beer and gently stir. Fold in flour until just combined.

3. Dip halibut chunks in batter and deep-fry until golden brown and done inside. To maintain oil temperature, avoid overloading fryer. Serve hot with tartar sauce.

SEAFOOD

Pan-Seared Pecan Cod

Panko crumbs and pecans give a delicate, crunchy coating to mild cod. But unlike many recipes for breaded fish, this one doesn't require deep-frying.

Makes 4 servings

½ cup panko bread crumbs

½ cup finely chopped pecans

⅓ cup all-purpose flour

1 teaspoon baking powder

½ teaspoon salt

½ teaspoon freshly ground black pepper

½ teaspoon paprika

½ cup buttermilk

1½ pounds true cod fillets, about 3 ounces each

1 tablespoon butter

1 lemon, cut into wedges, for serving

1. In a shallow dish, combine panko crumbs and pecans.

2. In another shallow dish, combine flour, baking powder, salt, pepper, and paprika; mix well.

3. In a third shallow dish, add buttermilk.

4. Working with one fish fillet at a time, dust in flour mixture and shake off excess. Dip fillet in buttermilk to evenly coat and drain excess. Dredge in pecan mixture, coating thoroughly.

5. In a large skillet, heat butter over medium heat; add fillets and cook on each side for 2 to 3 minutes or until golden, and fish flakes with a fork. Serve with lemon wedges.

SEAFOOD

Mahi Mahi with Mango Salsa

Mango salsa, fragrant with ginger and lime, balances the richness of mahi mahi. This dish works nicely on the grill as well as in a skillet.

Makes 4 servings

1 teaspoon rice wine vinegar

3 tablespoons olive oil, divided

1 tablespoon honey

1 lime, juiced

Salt and freshly ground black pepper

1 large mango, pitted, peeled, and finely diced

2 tablespoons chopped fresh cilantro

2 green onions, chopped

1 clove garlic, minced

2 teaspoons peeled and minced fresh ginger

1½ pounds mahi mahi fillets

1. In a large bowl, whisk together vinegar, 1 tablespoon oil, the honey, lime juice, ¼ teaspoon salt, and ½ teaspoon pepper. Add the mango, cilantro, green onions, garlic, and ginger; mix and set aside.

2. Heat a large skillet over medium-high heat. Brush the mahi mahi fillets with the remaining 2 tablespoons oil, and season with salt and pepper. Fry fish, turning once, just until opaque in the thickest part, 6 to 8 minutes, or until an instant-read thermometer inserted in thickest part of fish measures 145°F

3. Serve mahi mahi with mango salsa.

SEAFOOD

Pistachio-Lime Sea Scallops

This is such a simple yet sublime way to prepare scallops. The succulent scallops are rolled in a vibrant mixture of lime zest, chives, and pistachios after they are cooked. I usually serve this as an appetizer, but it can also be a lovely main course.

Makes 2 to 3 servings

3 tablespoons butter, divided

¼ cup finely chopped unsalted pistachios

1 tablespoon vegetable oil

1 pound sea scallops

2 tablespoons finely chopped fresh chives

1 tablespoon finely grated lime zest

Freshly ground black pepper

1 lime, juiced

1. In a large skillet, heat 1 tablespoon butter over medium heat. Add pistachios and sauté for 2 minutes. Remove nuts to a small bowl and set aside.

2. To the same skillet, add remaining 2 tablespoons butter and 1 tablespoon oil; heat over medium-high. Add scallops and cook, turning once, until browned and opaque, about 6 minutes. Remove scallops.

3. Meanwhile, add chives, lime zest, and pepper to taste to pistachios; mix well. Roll hot scallops in nut mixture, pour lime juice over top, and serve.

Classic Crab Louis

I first enjoyed this salad after I moved to the Northwest, where it quickly became one of my favorites. It makes a wonderful starter or a satisfying meal.

3 hard-cooked eggs, divided

1 cup mayonnaise (preferably a brand made with olive oil)

¼ cup cocktail or chili sauce

1 teaspoon fresh lemon juice

1 tablespoon minced shallot

½ teaspoon Worcestershire sauce

2 teaspoons minced fresh Italian (flat-leaf) parsley

½ head romaine lettuce, shredded

1 pound shelled crab meat

2 tomatoes, cut into wedges, for garnish

Capers, for garnish

1. Slice two hard-cooked eggs and set aside.

2. Chop remaining hard-cooked egg and add to a large bowl. Add mayonnaise, cocktail sauce, lemon juice, shallot, Worcestershire sauce, and parsley; mix gently and set aside.

3. On individual plates, make a bed of shredded lettuce and mound crab meat in the middle. Top with dressing. Garnish with tomatoes and sliced eggs. Place capers around the edges and serve.

SEAFOOD

Clams Steamed in Wine, Garlic, and Oregano

Clams are such a great quick meal—especially when you steam them in a fragrant broth of butter, wine and a few seasonings. You'll definitely want lots of crusty bread for sopping up the delicious broth.

Makes 6 servings

½ cup butter (1 stick)

5 cloves garlic, minced

2½ cups dry white wine

1 tablespoon dried oregano

2 tablespoons chopped fresh Italian (flat-leaf) parsley

1 teaspoon crushed red pepper flakes

2 pounds in-shell Manila clams, scrubbed

1. In a large skillet, melt butter over medium heat. Add garlic and sauté just until fragrant, about 30 seconds. Stir in wine, oregano, parsley, and red pepper flakes. Bring to a boil.

2. Add clams to wine mixture; cover and steam until all the clams have opened, about 6 minutes. Discard any that do not open. Serve in soup bowls, and ladle broth generously over them.

Coconut-Lemongrass-Lime Shrimp

Lemongrass, ginger, curry powder, and hot chili paste make a sensational marinade for any seafood. Here I use it for shrimp, and then serve the flavorful marinade as a warm dipping sauce.

Makes 4 servings

Wooden skewers

1½ tablespoons finely grated lemongrass

3 cloves garlic, minced

2 tablespoons peeled and minced fresh ginger

1 (14-ounce) can light coconut milk

Finely grated zest from 1 lime

2 tablespoons lime juice

1 teaspoon hot chili paste

1 tablespoon curry powder

1 tablespoon firmly packed brown sugar

2 pounds large wild shrimp, peeled,
   with the tails left on

1. Soak wooden skewers in water for 30 minutes.

2. Meanwhile, in a medium bowl, add lemongrass, garlic, ginger, coconut milk, lime zest, lime juice, chili paste, curry powder, and brown sugar; mix well.

3. Thread two skewers into one shrimp, one at the tail and the other near the head. Lay in a glass dish and repeat with remaining shrimp. Pour half of the marinade over the shrimp. Put remaining marinade in a small saucepan and set aside. Turn skewers to coat shrimp well, cover, and refrigerate for 30 minutes.

4. Preheat the grill to high heat. Meanwhile, heat reserved marinade over low heat.

5. Place the skewers on grill, close the lid and cook for 3 minutes. Turn skewers, close lid, and cook for 3 more minutes. Remove shrimp from grill and serve with warm marinade for dipping.

SEAFOOD

Shrimp Tacos with Avocado Salsa

Seafood tacos are such a treat—especially when made with shrimp. Instead of serving them with a tomato-based salsa, I've made a fresh avocado salsa boosted with the flavor of toasted coriander and cumin.

Makes 4 to 6 servings

1¾ teaspoons ground cumin

¾ teaspoon ground coriander

2 pounds large wild shrimp, shelled and deveined

½ teaspoon cayenne pepper

½ teaspoon salt

½ teaspoon freshly ground black pepper

2 tablespoons olive oil

12 to 16 corn tortillas

2 large avocados, pitted, peeled, and cubed

1 teaspoon lime juice, plus wedges for serving

1 medium tomato

1 medium red bell pepper, cored, and finely chopped

1 medium red onion, finely chopped

3 tablespoons chopped fresh cilantro,
    plus sprigs for garnish

½ teaspoon hot pepper sauce

½ medium cabbage, finely shredded

1. In a small, dry skillet, heat coriander and cumin over medium heat. Cook, stirring, for 1 minute. Remove from heat and let cool.

2. In a medium bowl, add shrimp, 1 teaspoon of the toasted spices, the cayenne, salt, and pepper; toss well to combine.

3. In a large skillet, heat oil over medium-high heat. Add shrimp and sauté for 5 minutes, until opaque. Remove from skillet and keep warm.

4. In the same skillet, lightly heat tortillas on both sides and keep warm.

5. In a medium bowl, toss avocado with lime juice. Cut tomato in half and squeeze gently to remove seeds. Chop finely and add to avocado along with bell pepper, onion, cilantro, remaining toasted spices, and hot sauce; gently combine.

6. To serve, place shrimp in a tortilla, top with shredded cabbage and avocado salsa. Squeeze a lime wedge over the top. Garnish with cilantro sprigs and serve.

SEAFOOD

Quick Saffron Mussels with Shallots and Cream

Every time I prepare this easy dish, my husband asks why I don't serve it more often. As with my recipe for steamed clams, you'll want plenty of crusty bread to go with these mussels.

Makes 2 servings

6 tablespoons butter

2 medium shallots, thinly sliced

½ teaspoon saffron threads, crushed

2 cloves garlic, minced

1 cup dry white wine

½ cup heavy whipping cream

2 pounds in-shell mussels, rinsed well and debearded

3 tablespoons chopped fresh Italian (flat-leaf) parsley

2 teaspoons freshly ground black pepper

½ teaspoon salt

1. In a large stockpot, melt the butter over medium heat. Add the shallots, saffron, and garlic. Sauté for 3 minutes, or until shallots are translucent.

2. Add the wine and cream and bring to a boil. Add the mussels, stir, and cover. Cook for 3 minutes, or until the mussels open. Discard any that do not open.

3. Add parsley, salt, and pepper; stir gently. Serve in big bowls with crusty bread for dipping.

SEAFOOD

Rotisserie Chicken Sloppy Joes, page 102

Dijon Split Chicken, page 106

Mediterranean Artichoke Chicken, page 107

Yogurt-Lime Chicken Kebabs, page 109

Poultry

Tomato-Olive Chicken

Shallots, olives, and freshly squeezed lemon juice make plain chicken breast special.

Makes 4 servings

1 tablespoon olive oil

4 boneless, skinless chicken breasts

1 medium green bell pepper, cored and cut into 1-inch-wide strips

2 medium shallots, peeled and quartered

1 (14.5-ounce) can diced tomatoes, undrained

¼ cup pitted and sliced kalamata olives

½ cup chicken broth

1 teaspoon finely grated lemon zest

2 tablespoons fresh lemon juice

1 teaspoon dried oregano, crumbled

⅛ teaspoon ground cinnamon

¼ teaspoon salt

¼ teaspoon freshly ground black pepper

1. Heat a Dutch oven over medium-high heat. Add oil and cook the chicken for 2 minutes; turn and cook for 2 minutes more.

2. Add the bell pepper and shallots; cook for 2 to 3 minutes, or until the vegetables are tender-crisp, stirring occasionally.

3. Add tomatoes, olives, broth, lemon zest and juice, oregano, cinnamon, salt, and pepper; bring to a simmer. Cover and simmer for 15 minutes, or just until chicken is no longer translucent in the center, stirring occasionally.

POULTRY

Creamy Mustard Chicken

Shallots, apples, and Dijon mustard give basic chicken breasts a French accent. This dish is also quick enough to make after work, but special enough for guests.

Makes 4 to 6 servings

6 boneless, skinless chicken breasts
Salt and freshly ground black pepper
1 tablespoon vegetable oil
2 large shallots, chopped

2 Granny Smith apples, peeled, cored, and
　　sliced ½ inch thick
1 cup chicken broth
2 teaspoons cornstarch
2 tablespoons water
½ cup heavy whipping cream
¼ cup Dijon mustard
3 tablespoons chopped fresh Italian (flat-leaf) parsley

1. Season chicken with salt and pepper. In a large skillet with lid, heat oil over medium-high; add chicken and brown on both sides; remove from pan.

2. Add shallots to skillet and sauté over medium-high heat for about 2 minutes. Add apples and sauté for 2 minutes. Add broth.

3. In a small bowl, blend cornstarch in 2 tablespoons water; slowly whisk into chicken broth. Add cream and mustard and return chicken to pan; cover, reduce heat to medium, and cook just until chicken is no longer translucent inside, about 10 minutes.

4. Garnish with parsley and serve.

Chicken Tagine with Chutney

Whether or not you serve this in a traditional Moroccan tagine dish, the flavors of ginger, cinnamon, and leeks make it exotic.

Makes 4 servings

1 tablespoon olive oil

⅓ cup chopped onion

1 pound boneless, skinless chicken breasts, cubed (2-inch)

1 teaspoon peeled and finely grated fresh ginger

1 teaspoon ground cinnamon

2 cups chicken broth

1 leek, sliced in half lengthwise, rinsed well, and thinly cut crosswise

1 zucchini, diced (½-inch)

1 cup prepared chutney

Salt and freshly ground black pepper

4 to 6 cups hot cooked rice, for serving

1. In a large skillet, heat oil over medium heat. Add onion and sauté until translucent.

2. Add chicken and cook until golden on all sides. Add ginger, cinnamon, broth, and leek; bring to a boil. Reduce heat, cover, and simmer for 15 minutes.

3. Stir in zucchini and chutney; cook for 10 minutes. Remove from heat and season to taste with salt and pepper. Serve with hot rice.

POULTRY

Rotisserie Chicken Sloppy Joes

Making your own barbecue sandwich is a snap, especially when you use a fully cooked rotisserie chicken. And kids love this. Note that the sauce is also excellent on beef and pork, such as my Oh Baby! Baby Back Ribs.

Makes 4 to 6 servings

Sloppy Joes:

1 whole cooked chicken, meat pulled from
   bones and skin and shredded

6 kaiser rolls

Classic Barbecue Sauce:

1 cup ketchup

3 tablespoons firmly packed brown sugar

1 tablespoon dry mustard

1 tablespoon cider vinegar

2 teaspoons Worcestershire sauce

½ teaspoon salt

½ teaspoon freshly ground black pepper

½ teaspoon hot pepper sauce
   (add more or less per your "hotness" meter)

To make sauce:

1. In a large saucepan, add all sauce ingredients and bring to a boil over medium heat. Reduce heat and simmer for 10 minutes, stirring occasionally.

To make Sloppy Joes:

1. To the sauce add chicken and combine; cover and cook until heated throughout, 3 to 5 minutes.

2. Spoon ½ cup chicken mixture onto bottom half of each roll. Cover with roll tops and serve.

Tarragon-Grape-Chicken Salad

Chicken salad used to be a staple for ladies who lunch, but I've updated the classic by adding grapes, cashews, and tarragon. The result is sensational.

Makes 4 servings

2 cups chopped cooked chicken

1 cup green or red grapes, halved

1½ cups chopped celery

¾ cup chopped green onions

⅓ cup mayonnaise (preferably a brand made with olive oil)

1 tablespoon fresh lemon juice

2 teaspoons dried tarragon

Salt and freshly ground black pepper

Lettuce leaves or wedges of fresh tomato, for serving

Roasted cashews, for garnish

1. In a large bowl, add chicken, grapes, celery, green onions, mayonnaise, lemon juice, tarragon, and salt and pepper to taste; mix well.

2. Serve in lettuce cups or surrounded by tomato wedges, and garnish with cashews.

POULTRY

Caribbean Chicken and Squash Stew

Using a slow-cooker to make this recipe means that you can come home in the evening to a fragrant, tender chicken dinner.

Makes 4 to 6 servings

2 small butternut squash, peeled, seeded,
    and cut into 1½-inch pieces
1 (14.5-ounce) can diced tomatoes, undrained
2 medium onions, cut into wedges
⅓ cup chicken broth
1 teaspoon peeled and finely grated fresh ginger
1 tablespoon curry powder
1 teaspoon salt
3 pounds bone-in chicken parts
Hot cooked rice, for serving

1. In a slow-cooker, combine squash, tomatoes, onions, broth, ginger, curry powder, and salt; mix well. Place chicken on top of vegetable mixture and cook on high setting for 3 to 4 hours, or on low for 7 to 8 hours.

2. Remove chicken from slow-cooker and cool slightly. Pull meat from skin and bones and return to pot. Stir well to combine and serve with hot rice.

POULTRY

Dijon Split Chicken

Cutting a chicken in half speeds up the cooking, and adding broth at the end of roasting creates a flavorful sauce.

Makes 2 servings

1 whole 3- to 4-pound chicken, halved

½ teaspoon salt

½ teaspoon freshly ground black pepper

3 tablespoons olive oil

2 tablespoons butter, melted

1 teaspoon Worcestershire sauce

2 teaspoons fresh rosemary

3 tablespoons Dijon mustard

½ cup chicken broth

2 tablespoons chopped fresh Italian (flat-leaf) parsley

1. Season chicken with salt and pepper.

2. In a medium bowl, mix oil, butter, Worcestershire sauce, rosemary, and mustard. Rub the chicken on all sides with mixture. Place chicken in a roasting pan and refrigerate for 30 minutes.

3. Preheat oven to 375°F.

4. Bake chicken for 30 minutes. Remove pan from oven, add broth, and gently stir. Bake for 10 minutes more, or until an instant-read thermometer inserted in the thickest part of the thigh registers 165°F.

5. Sprinkle chicken with parsley and serve with juices.

Mediterranean Artichoke Chicken

This is another quick recipe that can be made with rotisserie chicken.

Makes 4 servings

1 cup chicken broth

4 green onions, sliced

1 tablespoon butter

1 clove garlic, minced

¾ cup couscous

2 tablespoons olive oil

½ red bell pepper, cored and chopped

3 cups shredded cooked chicken

1 cup frozen artichoke hearts

1 teaspoon dried oregano

½ cup kalamata olives, pitted and halved, for serving

1 ounce feta cheese, crumbled (¼ cup), for serving

1. In a small saucepan, combine broth, green onions, butter, and garlic; bring to a boil. Stir in couscous. Remove from heat and let stand, covered, for 5 minutes.

2. Heat 2 tablespoons olive oil in a large skillet with lid; add bell pepper and sauté for 2 minutes. Stir in chicken, artichoke hearts, and oregano;

cover and cook for 5 minutes, or until heated through.

3. Divide couscous mixture among four plates. Top with chicken mixture, sprinkle with olives and cheese, and serve.

POULTRY

Herb-Rubbed Cornish Game Hens

Game hens are so easy to cook, and they make a meal feel really special. So be brave and give them a try. Two birds are perfect for two people.

2 servings

2 Cornish game hens

1 tablespoon butter

¼ cup finely chopped fresh herbs, such as thyme, rosemary, and sage, plus extra sprigs for stuffing cavity and garnish

Salt and freshly ground black pepper

1. Preheat oven to 400°F.

2. In a large, shallow roasting pan, add hens. If there are any giblets inside hens, remove them. Rub hens with butter.

3. In a small bowl, combine chopped herbs and salt and pepper to taste. Rub hens inside and out with herb mixture. Place herb sprigs in hens' cavities.

4. Roast for 50 to 55 minutes, or until an instant-read thermometer inserted in the thickest part of the thigh registers 165°F.

5. Remove hens from the pan and let rest 10 minutes.

Yogurt-Lime Chicken Kebabs

These fragrant kebabs use thigh meat, which is juicier and more flavorful than breast meat.

Makes 4 servings

1 cup plain Greek yogurt (low-fat or full-fat)

2 cloves garlic, minced

1 lime, zested and juiced

1 tablespoon ground cumin

1 teaspoon paprika

½ teaspoon cayenne pepper

Salt and freshly ground black pepper

1½ pounds boneless, skinless chicken thighs,
    cut into 2-inch pieces

Metal skewers

1. In a large glass bowl, add yogurt, garlic, lime juice and zest, cumin, paprika, cayenne, and salt and pepper to taste. Add chicken and marinate in refrigerator for 1 to 4 hours.

2. Preheat oven to broil. Thread chicken onto metal skewers. Broil kebabs for 6 for 8 minutes, or until cooked through and browned.

POULTRY

Creamy Avocado Chicken Sliders

Once you try this amazing version of chicken salad, you'll never go back. The yogurt and avocado make the filling incredibly creamy. And just for the record, I prefer the richer flavor of mayonnaise made with olive oil.

Makes 4 to 6 servings

4 cups cooked chicken, chopped or shredded

4 green onions, chopped

1 jalapeño chile, seeded and chopped

¼ cup plain Greek yogurt (low-fat or full-fat)

2 tablespoons mayonnaise
    (preferably a brand made with olive oil)

2 tablespoons fresh lime juice

Salt and freshly ground black pepper

Slider buns or other small rolls

3 avocados

Fresh cilantro sprigs

1. In a large bowl, combine chicken, green onions, jalapeño, yogurt, mayonnaise, and lime juice. Season to taste with salt and pepper. Refrigerate until serving time.

2. When you're ready to serve sliders, pit, peel, and mash avocados; stir into chicken mixture. Divide filling among bottom halves of buns, top with a sprig of cilantro, then add tops of buns and serve.

Turkey-Orzo Stuffed Peppers

Here's a simple spin on stuffed peppers using orange instead of green peppers, and turkey and orzo instead of rice and beef.

Makes 4 to 6 servings

⅓ cup orzo pasta

1 tablespoon olive oil

½ small onion, chopped

1 pound ground turkey

¼ cup water

3 tablespoons chopped fresh dill, divided

Salt and freshly ground black pepper

4 medium tomatoes, coarsely chopped

3 orange bell peppers, stem intact, halved lengthwise
through stem, ribs and seeds discarded

1. Preheat oven to 425°F.

2. Cook pasta in boiling salted water until al dente; drain and return to pot.

3. In a large skillet, heat oil over medium heat. Add onion and sauté until softened. Spread half the onion in a lightly oiled baking dish.

4. Add ground turkey to remaining onion in skillet and cook about 3 minutes. Remove from heat and stir in cooked orzo, ¼ cup water, 2½ tablespoons dill, ½ teaspoon salt, and ½ teaspoon pepper.

5. Stir tomatoes into onion in pie plate and season with salt and pepper to taste. Place bell pepper halves, cut sides up, in tomato-onion mixture. Fill pepper halves with turkey mixture, cover baking dish with foil and bake 20 minutes. Remove foil and bake another 10 minutes.

6. Garnish with tomato-onion mixture and remaining ½ tablespoon dill, and serve.

POULTRY

Knife-and-Fork Corned Beef Reuben, page 123

Roast Prime Rib, page 125

Pork Tenderloin with Coffee-Chili Rub, page 126

Lemon-Herb Grilled Lamb Chops, page 129

Meat

Sunday Pot Roast

This traditional pot roast braises to perfection and is even better served the next day.

4 pounds boneless beef chuck roast, cut into 4- to
    5-inch pieces

3 tablespoons olive oil, divided

½ teaspoon salt

Freshly ground black pepper

2 large onions, thinly sliced

3 medium potatoes, peeled and cubed

4 carrots, peeled and chopped

2 stalks celery, chopped

2 cups dry red wine

1 tablespoon Worcestershire sauce

2 tablespoons all-purpose flour

½ cup water

1. Preheat oven to 300°F.

2. In a large bowl, add roast and 1 tablespoon oil; turn meat to coat with oil. Generously sprinkle meat all over with salt and pepper.

3. Heat a Dutch oven over medium heat. Add remaining 2 tablespoons oil and brown roast pieces, 4 to 5 minutes per side. Remove meat to a baking sheet.

4. Add onions to Dutch oven and cook until soft and golden, 4 to 5 minutes. Add potatoes, carrots, celery, wine, and Worcestershire sauce; bring to a simmer and remove from heat.

5. Return pot roast to Dutch oven, cover, and bake until roast is tender, 2 to 2½ hours.

6. Remove lid and transfer meat and vegetables to baking sheet. Heat pan drippings over medium-high heat. Mix flour with ½ cup of water and add to drippings; simmer until slightly thickened, about 3 minutes. Serve immediately with juices.

Flat-Iron Steak with Chimichurri Sauce

Flat-iron is an amazingly tender cut of beef and a snap to prepare. Pair it with this tangy Argentine sauce for an amazing meal. The bright flavors of the chimichurri, aided by lots of garlic, really transform ordinary steak.

Makes 4 to 6 servings

2 pounds flat-iron, flank, or skirt steak

¾ cup olive oil, plus 1 tablespoon, divided

Salt and freshly ground black pepper

1 cup coarsely chopped fresh Italian (flat-leaf) parsley

½ cup coarsely chopped fresh cilantro

¼ cup garlic cloves (about 10)

⅓ cup red wine vinegar

2 tablespoons dried oregano

1 teaspoon ground cumin

1. Heat a large skillet to medium-high heat. Brush steak with 1 tablespoon olive oil, then season to taste with salt and pepper. Add steak to skillet and cook to desired doneness, 4 to 5 minutes per side for medium-rare. Transfer to a plate, tent with foil and let rest for 5 minutes.

2. Meanwhile, in a blender or food processor, add the parsley, cilantro, remaining ¾ cup olive oil, the garlic, vinegar, oregano, cumin, and 1 teaspoon salt. Blend until ingredients are evenly chopped.

3. Slice the steak thinly across the grain and arrange on a serving platter. Pour a little of the chimichurri over top, and serve extra on the side.

Quick Beef Burgundy

This is a faster version of the classic. Start with a great cut of meat, season with sage, and serve with egg noodles. By the time the noodles are done cooking the dish is ready to be served.

Makes 2 to 3 servings

12 ounces wide egg noodles

1 pound New York strip steak, cut into 1-inch pieces

Salt and freshly ground black pepper

2 tablespoons butter, divided

12 ounces fresh mushrooms, sliced

2 large shallots, sliced

1 teaspoon finely chopped fresh thyme, plus sprigs for garnish

1 teaspoon dried sage

½ cup dry red wine

1 cup beef broth

1 (14.5-ounce) can diced tomatoes, undrained

1. Cook noodles in boiling salted water until al dente; drain and keep warm.

2. Season beef with salt and pepper to taste.

3. In a large skillet, melt 1 tablespoon butter over medium-high heat. Add beef and brown on all sides, about 3 minutes. Remove beef from skillet.

4. Melt remaining 1 tablespoon butter in same skillet over medium-high heat. Add mushrooms and shallots; sauté until vegetables soften, about 5 minutes. Stir in thyme, sage, wine, broth, and tomatoes. Increase heat and boil until sauce is reduced and thickened, about 8 minutes.

5. Return beef and juices to skillet. Cook about 1 minute. Serve over noodles and garnish with thyme sprigs.

Slow-Cooker Swiss Steak

This is the ultimate in comfort food, especially when served with your favorite side, such as mashed potatoes or the Creamy Colcannon on page 175. You'll want to hibernate for the winter after this meal.

Makes 6 to 8 servings

2 tablespoons all-purpose flour

½ teaspoon salt

¼ teaspoon freshly ground black pepper

2 pounds round steak

2 tablespoons butter

½ cup chopped onion

1 (14.5-ounce) can stewed tomatoes, undrained

½ cup water

2 teaspoons red wine vinegar

1. In a small bowl, combine flour, salt, and pepper; rub mixture on steak.

2. In a large skillet, melt butter over medium-high heat. Add steak and chopped onion; cook, stirring onions occasionally, until meat is browned on both sides, about 5 minutes.

3. Transfer meat and onions to a slow-cooker. Add tomatoes, ½ cup water and the vinegar. Cover and cook on low for 6 to 8 hours, or on high for 3 to 4 hours.

Knife-and-Fork Corned Beef Reuben

This is an old-school—and very messy—sandwich, which is why you may want to eat it with a knife and fork. Do yourself a favor and make your own corned beef; the instructions are right on the meat package and it's very easy.

Makes 4 servings

2 cups fresh (refrigerated) sauerkraut, undrained

8 slices rye bread

2 tablespoons butter, at room temperature

½ cup Thousand Island dressing

8 slices gruyère or swiss cheese

1 pound cooked corned beef, sliced

1. In a small pan, heat sauerkraut and juices; keep warm.

2. Heat a large skillet over medium heat. Butter each bread slice on one side.

3. Place 2 slices of bread, buttered side down, in skillet. Spread a layer of Thousand Island dressing on both slices. Using a slotted spoon, remove a quarter of the sauerkraut and press out liquid. Spread evenly over the dressing on one slice of bread. Arrange two slices of cheese and a quarter of the corned beef in an even layer over the sauerkraut. Place the other slice of bread, buttered side up, over the corned beef. Repeat for second sandwich.

4. Cook until the bread is browned. Turn the sandwiches over and brown the other side. Repeat with remaining 4 bread slices and fillings. Serve immediately.

Dijon-Roasted Rack of Pork

A rack of pork makes an impressive meal when carved at the table. The mustard and herbed coating adds succulent flavor to this delicious cut of meat.

Makes 4 to 6 servings

¾ cup minced fresh Italian (flat-leaf) parsley

5 cloves garlic, minced

1 tablespoon dried thyme, crumbled

1 tablespoon dried sage

1 (3- to 4-pound) pork rib rack roast

Salt and freshly ground black pepper

¼ cup Dijon mustard

1. Preheat oven to 350°F.

2. In medium bowl, combine parsley, garlic, thyme, and sage. Season pork on all sides with salt and pepper; brush all over with mustard. Sprinkle herb mixture over pork and place rounded side up in a shallow roasting pan.

3. Roast 1½ hours or until instant-read thermometer inserted into center of meat reaches 140°F (medium doneness). Remove from oven, tent meat with foil, and let rest for 10 minutes before carving.

Roast Prime Rib

Don't be intimidated by prime rib. If you use an instant-read thermometer you can't go wrong. Just be sure to allow time for the roast to rest after it comes out of the oven. This allows the juices to redistribute throughout the meat. Be sure to buy a prime rib roast that has had the bones cut off and then tied back onto the meat.

Makes 8 servings

1 (8- to 9-pound) prime rib beef roast
Salt
3 tablespoons Dijon mustard
3 cloves garlic, minced
2 tablespoons coarsely ground black pepper
1 tablespoon butter
2 large shallots, minced
3½ cups beef broth
⅓ cup dry red wine
Prepared horseradish, for serving

1. Preheat oven to 450°F.

2. Place beef, fat side up, on a rimmed baking sheet. Sprinkle with salt. Mix mustard and garlic together and spread on top of beef. Sprinkle pepper over mustard mixture. Roast beef for 15 minutes.

3. Reduce oven temperature to 325°F. Roast until an instant-read thermometer inserted into center of beef measures 125°F (medium-rare), about 2 hours, 45 minutes. Transfer roast to platter, tent loosely with foil, and let rest for 20 minutes before carving.

4. Meanwhile, pour off pan juices into a bowl, including any browned bits you can scrape up from bottom of pan; set aside.

5. In a skillet, melt butter over medium heat. Add shallots and sauté until tender. Add beef broth and wine; boil until liquid is reduced by half, about 15 minutes. Add reserved pan juices. Serve roast with horseradish.

Pork Tenderloin with Coffee-Chili Rub

Cocoa, chili powder, and coffee add layers of complexity to pork. Since a tenderloin is a very lean cut of meat, be careful not to overcook it.

Makes 4 servings

¼ cup finely ground coffee (espresso grind)

2 tablespoons unsweetened cocoa powder

1 tablespoon firmly packed dark brown sugar

2 teaspoons salt

2 teaspoons freshly ground black pepper

2 teaspoons ground cumin

1 teaspoon chili powder

½ teaspoon allspice

½ teaspoon ground cinnamon

½ teaspoon cayenne pepper

½ teaspoon paprika

2 pork tenderloins, tied together

2 tablespoons olive oil

1. On a large plate, combine coffee, cocoa powder, brown sugar, salt, black pepper, cumin, chili powder, allspice, cinnamon, cayenne, and paprika. Roll pork in spice mixture, pressing, until meat is completely covered. Let rest for at least 1 hour or up to overnight.

2. Preheat oven to 350°F.

3. In a large skillet or grill pan, heat oil over medium-high heat. Place tenderloin in pan and brown for 3 to 4 minutes; turn meat and continue to cook and turn until all sides are browned.

4. Place pork in a roasting pan. Bake for 25 to 30 minutes, or until an instant-read thermometer inserted in the center of the meat reaches 140 degrees. Remove pan from oven, tent meat with foil, and allow to rest for 8 to 10 minutes before slicing.

Spare Ribs and Sauerkraut

Brown sugar and applesauce lend a hint of sweetness that makes these ribs magnificent. They can be made in a Dutch oven or a slow-cooker.

Makes 4 servings

2 tablespoons vegetable oil

4 pounds pork spare ribs

Salt and freshly ground black pepper

3 pounds fresh (refrigerated) sauerkraut, drained

1 small onion, thinly sliced

2 cloves garlic, minced

1 tablespoon caraway seeds

2 tablespoons firmly packed brown sugar

2 cups applesauce

1. If using an oven, preheat to 325°F.

2. In a skillet, heat the oil over medium-high heat. Lightly season ribs with salt and pepper and brown in the skillet.

3. In a large bowl, mix the sauerkraut, onion, garlic, caraway seeds, 1 tablespoon pepper, the brown sugar, and applesauce. Layer the ribs and sauerkraut mixture in a slow-cooker or Dutch oven. For slow cooker, cover and cook on low setting for about 8 hours. If using oven, bake for 2 hours.

Spicy Orange Country-Style Ribs

These ribs have a nice balance of sweet and heat. But depending on who's coming for dinner, I'll turn up the heat with more hot chili paste.

Makes 4 servings

4 pounds bone-in country-style pork ribs

½ cup chili sauce

½ cup orange marmalade

1 teaspoon dark sesame oil

2 tablespoons rice vinegar

1 teaspoon hot chili paste

1 tablespoon reduced-sodium soy sauce

1 teaspoon olive oil

1. Preheat oven to 350°F.

2. Line a shallow baking pan with foil and add ribs. Cover with another piece of foil and bake for 1 hour.

3. Meanwhile, in a medium bowl, mix chili sauce, marmalade, sesame oil, vinegar, chili paste, soy sauce, and olive oil.

4. Remove ribs from oven and remove foil. Drain ribs well and pat dry. Turn oven setting to broil. Slather ribs with half of sauce. Broil for 5 minutes; turn ribs, baste, and broil for another 5 to 7 minutes. Serve with remaining sauce on the side.

Lemon-Herb Grilled Lamb Chops

In the summer, my friends stand around and eat these chops hot off the grill, holding them with their hands like "lamb" Popsicles.

Makes 2 to 3 servings

2 lemons, juiced

2 cloves garlic, crushed

1 teaspoon chopped fresh rosemary

1 tablespoon dried oregano

3 tablespoons olive oil

Salt and freshly ground black pepper

2 pounds lamb loin or rib chops

1. In a large bowl, mix lemon juice, garlic, rosemary, oregano, oil, and salt and pepper to taste. Add lamb chops and refrigerate 3 hours or up to overnight.

2. Preheat grill to medium-high heat. Remove lamb from marinade and place on grill. Close lid and grill for 4 minutes. Turn chops, close lid, and cook until an instant-read thermometer inserted in the thickest part of the meat measures 145°F (medium-rare). Remove chops from grill, tent loosely with foil and let rest for 5 minutes before serving.

Pork Kebabs with Cilantro-Yogurt Sauce

Lemongrass and garlic flavor this succulent pork that's complemented with a tangy cilantro-yogurt sauce. For a delicious gyro, serve the pork in pita bread with fresh tomato.

Makes 4 to 6 servings

2 tablespoons olive oil

1 tablespoon plus 1 teaspoon minced garlic, divided

1 tablespoon finely grated lemongrass

Salt and freshly ground black pepper

2 pounds pork loin, cut into 2-inch cubes

Wooden skewers

1 cup plain Greek yogurt (low-fat or full-fat)

2 tablespoons minced fresh cilantro

1 tablespoon minced fresh dill

1 lemon, cut into wedges, for serving

1. In a large bowl, mix olive oil, 1 tablespoon garlic, the lemongrass, 1 teaspoon salt, and pepper to taste. Add pork, toss and refrigerate for 2 hours or up to overnight.

2. Soak wooden skewers in water for 30 minutes.

3. Meanwhile, in a medium bowl, mix yogurt, cilantro, remaining 1 teaspoon garlic, the dill, and salt and pepper to taste.

4. Preheat oven to broil. Remove pork from marinade and thread on skewers. Broil kebabs for 6 to 8 minutes, or until done to your liking. Serve with yogurt sauce and lemon wedges.

Oh Baby! Baby Back Ribs

Tender baby back ribs in an hour and 10 minutes?
You bet—and mouthwateringly delicious, too.

Makes 3 to 4 servings

Barbecue Rub:

3 tablespoons firmly packed brown sugar

3 tablespoons paprika

2 tablespoons chili powder

2 tablespoons ground cumin

2 tablespoons kosher salt

1 tablespoon freshly ground black pepper

1 teaspoon freshly ground white pepper

Ribs:

2 racks baby back ribs

1 recipe Barbecue Sauce (see Rotisserie Chicken
    Sloppy Joes, page 102)

To make rub:

1. In a small bowl combine all seasonings and spices.

To make ribs:

1. Preheat grill to medium.

2. Pull the membrane from the back side of the
ribs (it helps to grip the edge of the membrane with
a paper towel). Coat both sides of ribs with rub,
pressing into the meat.

3. Cut both racks in half. Wrap each half rack tightly
in foil. Repeat so that ribs are double-sealed in foil.

4. Place packages on grill and close lid. After 30
minutes, carefully turn ribs over, close lid, and cook
for another 30 minutes. Remove ribs from grill and
carefully remove foil.

5. Place ribs back on grill and brush sparingly with
barbecue sauce. Turn and repeat. Close lid and cook
8 to 10 minutes, turning once and being careful not
to let ribs burn. Rest 5 minutes before serving.

Lamb Kebabs and Minty Vegetable Couscous

These versatile kebabs can be prepared under the broiler or on the grill, depending on the season. Try serving them with my Tzatziki on page 7.

Makes 4 to 6 servings

Wooden skewers

1⅓ cups vegetable or chicken broth

¾ cup couscous

2 pounds lamb, cut into 2-inch cubes

2 cloves garlic, minced

2 onions, cut into wedges

1 bunch green onions, finely chopped

1 red bell pepper, cored, seeded, and chopped

1 English cucumber, unpeeled, finely diced

2 tablespoons olive oil

1 tablespoon chopped fresh mint

Lemon wedges, for serving

1. Preheat broiler. Soak skewers in water for 30 minutes.

2. Meanwhile, in a medium saucepan bring broth to a boil over high heat. Add couscous, stir, cover, and reduce heat to low; cook for 3 to 5 minutes, or until all of the broth is absorbed.

3. Mix lamb with minced garlic. Skewer lamb cubes alternately with onion. Broil, turning once, until done to your liking.

4. Fluff up couscous with a fork, then stir in green onions, red pepper, cucumber, oil, and mint.

5. To serve, place lamb skewers on top of couscous and serve with lemon wedges.

Greek Leg of Lamb and Lemony Potatoes

This meal is perfect for Easter or Sunday dinner. The delicious lemon potatoes are the perfect complement to the rich and tender lamb.

Makes 6 servings

Salt and freshly ground black pepper

1 (4-pound) boneless leg of lamb, rolled and tied

2 lemons, juiced, divided

⅓ cup olive oil, divided

6 cloves garlic, sliced in half

4 pounds large russet potatoes, peeled and wedged lengthwise

2 tablespoons chopped fresh oregano

1. Preheat oven to 350°F.

2. In a small bowl, mix 1 tablespoon salt and 1 tablespoon pepper. Using your hands, coat meat with 1 tablespoon lemon juice and 1 tablespoon olive oil. Make 12 small (1-inch) cuts in meat and place in a large roasting pan. Rub garlic halves in the salt and pepper mixture and insert them into the incisions. Season meat with additional salt and pepper.

3. Add potato wedges to roasting pan. Pour remaining 5 tablespoons oil and remaining lemon juice over the potatoes.

4. Roast for 1 hour, or until an instant-read thermometer inserted in the center of the meat reaches 140°F degrees (medium doneness), about 25 minutes per pound. Remove from oven, tent meat with foil and allow to rest for 10 to 15 minutes before carving.

Artichoke-Tomato-Feta Pizza, page 143

Walla Walla Grilled Havarti Tosti, page 144

Cheesy Polenta with Sautéed Kale, page 145

Portobello Sandwiches with Creamy Tarragon, page 147

Meatless Mains

Baked Yams with Tangy Dill Yogurt

Yams step front and center in this unusual recipe. The sweetness of the potatoes is a lovely foil for the tangy yogurt topping, made heartier with the addition of rice.

Makes 4 servings

4 large yams

½ cup plain yogurt

¾ cup warm cooked rice

1 teaspoon dried dill

Salt and freshly ground black pepper

4 lemon wedges, for serving

1. Preheat oven to 400°F.

2. Prick the potatoes with a fork. Wrap individually in foil and bake for 60 minutes, or until tender. Unwrap and slice each potato lengthwise and squeeze it open; set aside.

3. Meanwhile, in a medium bowl, combine yogurt and rice. Add dill and salt and pepper to taste.

4. Squeeze the juice of a lemon wedge over the flesh of each potato. Add yogurt topping and serve.

Caramelized Onion and Olive Tart

I love to serve this as an appetizer if I'm entertaining. But it can also make a lovely entrée when served with a green salad.

Makes 3 entrée servings

2 tablespoons olive oil

3 medium onions, thinly sliced (about 4 cups)

1 clove garlic, minced

½ teaspoon dried thyme

¼ teaspoon salt

1 (1-pound) ball fresh pizza dough

¼ cup finely grated parmesan cheese, divided

¼ cup kalamata olives, pitted and sliced lengthwise

1. Preheat oven to 400°F. Lightly grease a baking sheet.

2. In a large skillet, heat oil over medium heat. Add onions and cook for 15 minutes or until golden brown. Add garlic, thyme, and salt; sauté for 2 minutes.

3. Stretch or roll pizza dough into a thin circle or rectangle and place on prepared backing sheet. Sprinkle with half of the cheese and bake 3 minutes. Remove from oven, top with onions and olives. Sprinkle with remaining cheese and bake 10 to 12 minutes.

Artichoke-Tomato-Feta Pizza

Pizzas are really fun to make, and they're simple when you start with fresh dough purchased from the store. Instead of using a tomato-based pizza sauce, this one uses olive oil topped with lots of fresh vegetables.

Makes 4 servings

1 (1-pound) ball fresh pizza dough

2 tablespoons olive oil

2 cloves garlic, minced

1 teaspoon dried oregano

3 tablespoons shredded fresh basil

Salt and freshly ground black pepper

4 roma tomatoes, chopped

1 cup frozen, thawed and roughly chopped
      artichoke hearts

¾ cup sliced mushrooms

4 ounces feta cheese, crumbled (1 cup)

½ cup cored and thinly sliced red bell pepper

1. Preheat oven to 400°F. Lightly grease a baking sheet.

2. Stretch or roll pizza dough into a thin rectangle and place on prepared baking sheet. Bake for 5 minutes.

3. Brush dough with olive oil; sprinkle with garlic, oregano, basil, and salt and pepper to taste. Drain any liquid from tomatoes. Scatter over pizza, along with artichoke hearts and mushrooms. Sprinkle with feta and bell pepper.

4. Bake 6 to 10 minutes, until crust is golden brown.

Walla Walla Grilled Havarti Tosti

We all love super sweet Walla Walla onions. Caramelized onions and creamy havarti cheese makes this the ultimate grown-up grilled cheese. If Walla Wallas aren't in season, use regular yellow onions.

Makes 4 servings

1 tablespoon olive oil
1 medium Walla Walla onion, chopped
½ teaspoon salt
½ teaspoon freshly ground black pepper
1 tablespoon butter, room temperature
8 slices artisan bread
8 ounces havarti cheese, coarsely grated, divided

1. In a large skillet, heat oil over low heat. Add onions and sauté until golden brown, about 20 minutes. Stir in salt and pepper and transfer to a bowl.

2. Lightly butter one side of each bread slice. Reserve ½ cup cheese for Step 3. Place the same skillet you used to cook the onions over medium heat. Place two slices of bread in skillet, buttered sides down. Top with one quarter of the Walla Walla onions, a handful of cheese and top with another slice of bread, buttered side up. Cook sandwiches, flipping once; about 2 minutes per side. Repeat with remaining bread, onions, and cheese.

3. Working with two sandwiches at a time, push sandwiches aside in skillet. Sprinkle a tablespoon of the reserved cheese in skillet. Lay one of the sandwiches directly onto the cheese. Repeat with second sandwich. Heat 2 minutes, until the cheese has slightly browned onto the bread. Repeat with second side.

Cheesy Polenta with Sautéed Kale

This dish is simple yet so satisfying. I have served this as an appetizer, side dish, and as a meal. If you're serving this as an appetizer, cut the polenta into bite-sized pieces.

Makes 4 entrée servings

¼ cup butter

2 cloves garlic, minced

4 cups reduced-sodium vegetable or chicken broth

1 cup polenta

7 ounces sharp cheddar or gouda cheese, coarsely grated

1 tablespoon olive oil

1 bunch kale, stemmed and thinly sliced crosswise

Salt and freshly ground black pepper

1 lemon, juiced

1. Butter a 9-by-13-inch baking dish.

2. In a medium saucepan, melt butter over medium-high heat. Add garlic and broth and heat until hot but not boiling. Reduce heat to low. Add polenta and cook, stirring frequently, for 10 minutes. Add the cheese and cook 5 minutes more. Pour into prepared baking dish and chill at least 1 hour. Cut into desired squares.

3. In a large skillet, heat oil over medium heat. Add kale and sauté for about 5 minutes. Season to taste with salt and pepper. Squeeze fresh lemon over top and toss. Transfer kale to a plate.

4. In the same skillet, heat the polenta squares over medium heat for a minute on each side. Serve topped with sautéed kale.

Quinoa-Stuffed Tomatoes with Summer Herbs

Protein-packed quinoa makes a delicious stuffing for fresh tomatoes. In summertime, I can easily make two pans of these. They're also delicious cold.

Makes 4 to 6 servings

6 to 8 large tomatoes

2 cups vegetable or chicken broth

1 cup quinoa

¼ cup chopped fresh basil

2 tablespoons chopped fresh mint

¼ teaspoon freshly ground black pepper

1. Preheat oven to 350°F.

2. Carefully cut stem and core out of tomatoes. Slice tops off the tomatoes and reserve. Scoop pulp out of the tomatoes, reserving pulp.

3. In a saucepan, bring broth to a boil over high heat. Stir in the quinoa, reduce heat to low, cover, and cook for 10 minutes. Remove from heat and gently stir in the basil, mint, pepper, and tomato pulp.

4. Place the tomato shells in a baking dish. Spoon the quinoa mixture into the shells, packing the mixture firmly. Place reserved tomato tops on top of stuffing and bake for 25 to 30 minutes or until heated through.

Portobello Sandwiches with Creamy Tarragon sauce

Meaty Portobello mushrooms make a fabulous substitute for beef. When combined with this special sauce, they make a winning sandwich.

Makes 4 servings

½ cup mayonnaise (preferably a brand made
with olive oil)

1 tablespoon finely chopped onion

2 teaspoons chopped fresh tarragon

2 tablespoons olive oil

4 large portobello mushrooms, stems removed and
gills scraped out

Salt and freshly ground black pepper

8 slices multi-grain bread

2 cups shredded iceberg lettuce

4 slices tomato

1. Preheat oven to broil.

2. In a small bowl, mix mayonnaise, onion, and tarragon; set aside.

3. Lightly brush olive oil on both sides of mushrooms and sprinkle with salt and pepper. Broil until tender, about 4 minutes per side.

4. Spread mayonnaise mixture on one side of each bread slice. Divide mushrooms, tomato slices, and lettuce among four slices of bread and top with remaining bread.

Spanakopita

This is a Greek spinach pie, made with feta and dill. I often crave this dish, and it's my second most requested recipe by friends, second only to Tzatziki. It works both as an entrée and an appetizer.

3 large eggs

2 tablespoons farina (such as Cream of Rice or Cream of Wheat cereal), uncooked

1½ cups finely chopped green onions

2 tablespoons chopped fresh dill

2 tablespoons chopped fresh Italian (flat-leaf) parsley

1 teaspoon salt

¼ teaspoon freshly ground black pepper

8 ounces feta cheese, crumbled (2 cups)

3 (10-ounce) packages frozen chopped spinach, thawed, water squeezed out with hands

8 ounces phyllo dough, thawed according to package directions

1 cup butter, melted (2 sticks)

1. Preheat oven to 350°F.

2. In a large bowl, mix eggs, farina, green onions, dill, parsley, salt, and pepper. Stir in feta and spinach.

3. Use a pastry brush and some of the melted butter to lightly grease a 9-by-13-inch baking pan. Carefully separate a sheet of phyllo dough and position it in the pan. Brush butter over phyllo. Repeat until you have layered and buttered 10 sheets of phyllo.

4. Spread filling evenly over phyllo. Layer remaining phyllo sheets, brushing each sheet with butter. Score pie through top layer of phyllo into desired serving pieces, but don't cut through the bottom layer yet. (Be sure to do this before baking or freezing. Pie can be frozen for 3 to 4 months.)

5. Bake pie for 35 to 40 minutes, or until golden brown. To serve, cut through scored lines down through bottom layer of phyllo.

Stuffed Squash with Pine Nuts, Raisins, and Brown Rice

This makes a superb meal with the addition of a cup of soup or a salad—especially my Fresh Greens, Orange, and Prosciutto Salad on page 51.

Makes 4 servings

3 tablespoons olive oil, divided

1 large shallot, finely chopped

5 green onions, chopped

4 cups cooked brown rice (prepared with vegetable broth instead of water)

¼ cup raisins

½ cup pine nuts, toasted

¼ cup chopped fresh parsley

1 teaspoon ground cumin

Dash hot pepper sauce

2 tablespoons dried dill

Salt and freshly ground black pepper

1 large egg, beaten

4 acorn or delicata squash, halved and seeded

2 ounces goat cheese, crumbled (½ cup)

1. Preheat oven to 350°F.

2. In a medium skillet, heat 1½ tablespoons oil over medium heat. Add shallot and green onions and sauté until translucent. Transfer mixture to a medium bowl. Add rice, raisins, pine nuts, parsley, cumin, hot pepper sauce, dill, and salt and pepper to taste; mix well. Let cool slightly and add egg. Mix gently and fill each squash half with stuffing. Drizzle with remaining 1½ tablespoons oil. Top with crumbled cheese.

3. Place on a rimmed baking sheet and bake for 45 minutes, until squash is tender when pierced with a fork.

Orzo Salad with Butternut Squash and Aged Cheddar

Roasting caramelizes vegetables, emphasizing their sweet, savory character. In this dish, I like roasting the squash and mushrooms separately so each retains its own individual flavor and adds layers of complexity to the dish.

Makes 4 to 6 servings

½ butternut squash, (about 1 pound), peeled, seeded, and cut into ½-inch cubes

5 tablespoons olive oil, divided

Salt and freshly ground black pepper

8 ounces portobello mushrooms, stemmed and gills scraped out

1 cup orzo pasta

4 cups water

2 tablespoons sherry vinegar

1 tablespoon fresh rosemary, finely chopped

½ cup thinly sliced green onions

7 ounces coarsely grated aged cheddar cheese (about 1¾ cups)

1. Preheat oven to 400°F.

2. In a baking pan, toss squash cubes with 2 teaspoons oil; season with salt and pepper.

3. Cut mushroom caps into 1-inch pieces. In a separate baking pan toss mushroom pieces with 1 teaspoon oil; season with salt and pepper. Place both baking pans in oven and roast until vegetables are tender, about 25 minutes for squash and 20 minutes for mushrooms.

4. Meanwhile, in a heavy-bottomed saucepan, heat 1 tablespoon oil over medium heat. Add orzo and cook for 5 minutes, stirring frequently, until it starts to brown. Add 4 cups water and ½ teaspoon salt and bring to a boil, stirring frequently. Reduce heat to low and simmer until pasta is al dente. Drain any excess water.

5. Transfer orzo to a mixing bowl and add remaining 3 tablespoons oil, the vinegar, and rosemary; mix well. Stir in green onions, squash, and mushrooms. Season to taste with salt and pepper and fold in cheese. Serve warm.

Eggplant Medallion Bolognese

Poor eggplant gets a bad rap, probably because it's usually fried—which it doesn't need. Baking is better, and leaves the vegetable with a more toothsome texture. It's even an easy dish to make on a weeknight.

1 cup seasoned dry bread crumbs

½ cup finely grated parmesan cheese

2 large eggs, beaten

1 tablespoon milk

⅓ cup all-purpose flour

1 large eggplant, cut crosswise into ½-inch slices

Olive oil spray or olive oil

1½ cups prepared marinara sauce

1½ cups coarsely grated mozzarella cheese

¼ cup coarsely chopped fresh basil

1. Preheat oven to 375°F. Cover a baking sheet with foil and lightly grease with oil.

2. In a shallow bowl or plate, combine bread crumbs with parmesan cheese. In another shallow bowl or pie plate, beat eggs with milk. Place flour on a large plate. Dredge eggplant slices in flour, then egg mixture, then bread crumbs. Place eggplant slices in single layer on prepared baking sheet.

3. Lightly spray or brush the tops of eggplant with olive oil. Bake about 20 minutes, until browned.

4. Meanwhile, in a saucepan, heat marinara sauce. Remove baking sheet from oven and turn eggplant over. Top slices with sauce, then mozzarella. Bake for 8 to 10 minutes, until cheese is melted and bubbly. Top with basil and serve.

Papoutsakia

In Greece, stuffed eggplant halves are called papoutsakia, or "little shoes." The original version has béchamel sauce on top, but this lighter version is topped with a little feta cheese.

4 large eggplants

2 tablespoons olive oil

1 cup finely chopped onion

1 (14.5-ounce) can diced tomatoes, drained, or 1 cup chopped fresh tomatoes

1½ cups cooked brown rice

2 tablespoons dried dill

2 cloves garlic, minced

½ cup chopped fresh Italian (flat-leaf) parsley

Salt and freshly ground black pepper

1 (14.5-ounce) can tomato sauce

1 teaspoon sugar

Crumbled feta cheese, for serving (optional)

1. Preheat oven to 350°F. Lightly grease a large casserole dish.

2. Pull outer leaves from stems of eggplant leaving stems attached. Cut eggplants in half lengthwise. Score the inside flesh with a knife, then remove flesh with a spoon, being careful not to rip eggplant skin. Chop the flesh.

3. In a large skillet, heat oil over medium heat. Add onion and sauté for 3 to 4 minutes. Add chopped eggplant and diced tomatoes; cook for 5 to 7 minutes. Add rice, dill, garlic, parsley, and salt and pepper to taste. Remove from heat.

4. Place eggplant halves in prepared casserole dish. Spoon filling into shells until they are heaping. Bake for 30 minutes.

5. Mix tomato sauce with sugar, and salt and pepper to taste. Remove casserole from oven and top with tomato sauce. Bake for another 30 minutes. If desired, top eggplant with crumbled feta 5 minutes before baking is done. Serve warm.

Roasted Root Vegetables, page 163

Summer Squash au Gratin, page 166

Sautéed Spinach with Chickpeas and Fresh Dill, page 167

Creamy Colcannon, page 175

Vegetables & Sides

Grilled Artichokes with Curried Dipping Sauce

There's something about sharing an artichoke that really gets the party started—even kids love them. When I'm grilling a meal, I do this appetizer on the grill, too. It's a fun and social way to begin an evening.

Makes 4 to 6 servings

4 artichokes

1 tablespoon olive oil

3 tablespoons mayonnaise (preferably a brand made with olive oil)

2 tablespoons Dijon mustard

½ teaspoon curry powder

Dash hot sauce

1. Using kitchen shears, trim the thorny tips from the artichoke leaves. Use a knife to slice about an inch off the top of the artichokes. Trim the end of the stalks and pull off any small outer leaves.

2. Place a steamer basket in a large pot and fill the bottom with several inches of water. Bring to a boil and add artichokes. Steam until outer leaves can easily be pulled off, about 25 minutes.

3. Remove artichokes from pot and let cool slightly. Slice in half, remove inner purple leaves, and gently scrape out fuzzy layer on top of the heart. Lightly brush with olive oil.

4. Preheat grill to medium heat. Grill artichokes about 2 minutes per side.

5. In a medium bowl, combine mayonnaise, mustard, curry powder, and hot sauce. Serve with grilled artichokes for dipping leaves.

Braised Celery Hearts

Who would have thought of celery as a side dish? Braising transforms this vegetable and gives it a nutty flavor and a tender texture.

Makes 4 to 6 servings

1 pound celery hearts

2 tablespoons butter

⅛ teaspoon salt

⅛ teaspoon freshly ground black pepper

1 cup chicken broth

1. Trim ends of celery ribs and slice crosswise into 2-inch lengths.

2. In a heavy skillet, melt butter over medium heat. Add celery and cook, stirring occasionally, until golden, about 8 minutes. Add salt, pepper, and broth; cover and cook until liquid has evaporated and celery is tender, about 20 minutes.

Roasted Root Vegetables

Adding rutabagas and turnips to the typical selection of potatoes, carrots, and onions make homey roasted vegetables special—especially in the fall when root vegetables are at the peak of the season.

Makes 8 servings

VEGETABLES & SIDES

2 cups peeled and cubed (2-inch) potato

1 cup peeled and sliced (2-inch) carrot

1 cup sliced (2-inch) parsnip

1 cup peeled and cubed (2-inch) rutabaga

1 cup peeled and cubed (2-inch) turnip

1 medium red onion, cut into large chunks

¾ cup chicken broth

2 to 3 tablespoons minced shallot

½ teaspoon dried thyme

3 tablespoons butter, cut into small pieces

1 lemon, juiced

Salt and freshly ground black pepper

1. Preheat oven to 350°F.

2. In a large baking pan, add potatoes, carrots, parsnips, rutabagas, turnips, onion, broth, shallot, thyme, and butter. Cover with foil and bake for about 25 minutes. Uncover and stir vegetables. Replace foil and cook another 20 minutes. Remove foil and let vegetables brown for another 10 minutes.

3. Remove pan from oven. Add lemon juice and season vegetables to taste with salt and pepper. Toss and serve.

Coconut-Chive Yams

Lime, two kinds of coconut, and chives make this a vibrant side dish that perks up plain chicken, chops, or fish. With a salad, the yams can also be the main attraction.

Makes 6 servings

6 yams, peeled and cubed

2 tablespoons olive oil

2 cups sour cream

¼ cup light coconut milk

1 cup unsweetened shredded dried coconut, toasted, divided

¼ cup chopped chives, divided

1 lime, juiced

1. Preheat oven to 400°F. Oil a large baking sheet.

2. Place yam cubes on prepared baking sheet. Roast 20 to 30 minutes, until yams are tender but not mushy.

3. Meanwhile, in a medium bowl, mix sour cream, coconut milk, ¾ cup toasted coconut, half of the chives, and all of the lime juice.

4. Serve potatoes topped with the sour cream mixture and garnish with remaining coconut and chives.

Simple Shaved Brussels Sprouts

Many people prepare Brussels sprouts with bacon or balsamic vinegar, but I find those ingredients aren't necessary when you shave the sprouts and quickly sauté them with a little olive oil and lemon juice.

Makes 6 servings

2 pounds fresh Brussels sprouts

1½ tablespoons olive oil

½ teaspoon salt

½ teaspoon freshly ground black pepper

½ lemon, juiced

1. Trim ends off the Brussels sprouts. Using a food processor fitted with the large slicing disk, shred sprouts.

2. In a large skillet, heat olive oil over medium-high heat. Add shredded sprouts and sauté 3 to 5 minutes. Add salt, pepper, and lemon juice; toss and serve.

Summer Squash au Gratin

My grandmother made a version of this when I was young. It's a great spin on the classic potatoes au gratin and can be made with any variety of summer squash.

Makes 4 to 6 servings

1 pound summer squash (such as zucchini or
    crookneck)
1 tablespoon olive oil
Dash salt
Dash freshly ground black pepper

¼ teaspoon dried thyme
1 (28-ounce) can crushed tomatoes, undrained
1 cup finely chopped onion
½ cup plain dried bread crumbs
1 tablespoon butter, melted
1 cup coarsely grated gruyère cheese

1. Trim squash and cut on the bias into ovals about ¼ inch thick. There should be about 5 cups.

2. In a large skillet, heat the oil over high heat. Add squash, salt, pepper, and thyme; cook about 2 minutes. Add tomatoes and onion; cover and cook 5 minutes, stirring occasionally.

3. Meanwhile, preheat oven to broil. Butter a 1½-quart baking dish.

4. Spoon squash into prepared baking dish. In a small bowl, combine bread crumbs and melted butter and scatter over squash. Top with cheese.

5. Place the dish under the broiler about 6 inches from the heat. Leave the door open and broil about 5 minutes or until golden brown on top. Serve hot.

Sautéed Spinach with Chickpeas and Fresh Dill

This is a quick dish that makes a tangy partner for grilled seafood. It can also be a meatless main course when served with crusty bread.

2 tablespoons olive oil

1 large onion, thinly sliced

1 (15.5-ounce) can chickpeas (garbanzo beans),
   drained and rinsed (1½ cups)

1 pound fresh baby spinach

½ cup minced fresh dill

2 lemons, juiced

Salt and freshly ground black pepper

1. In a large skillet, heat olive oil over medium heat. Add onion and sauté until soft. Add chickpeas and toss to coat in oil.

2. Add spinach and dill; cook until spinach is tender.

3. Stir in lemon juice, and season to taste with salt and pepper.

Manestra

This is a popular side dish of Greece. It's a delicious substitute for rice or potatoes—and it's a kid pleaser, too.

Makes 6 servings

1 pound orzo pasta

¾ cup coarsely grated mizithra cheese or crumbled feta cheese

¼ cup butter

¼ cup olive oil

Freshly ground black pepper

1. Cook the orzo in boiling salted water just until al dente. Drain, rinse in cold water, and drain again.

2. In a large skillet, heat butter and oil over medium-high heat. When butter smells fragrant and nutty, add the cooked orzo, reduce heat to low, and heat through.

3. Remove skillet from heat, add the cheese and season to taste with pepper; toss well and serve.

Sautéed Asparagus with Shallots and Lime

Shallots and lime are the perfect complement to fresh spring asparagus. Instead of grilling or broiling the spears, give them a quick turn in a hot skillet just until they are tender-crisp.

3 tablespoons butter

2 to 3 tablespoons minced shallot

1 pound fresh asparagus, trimmed

Salt and freshly ground black pepper

½ lime, juiced

1. In a large skillet, melt butter over medium heat. Add shallots and sauté for 2 minutes.

2. Add asparagus spears. Cover and cook 4 minutes, or just until tender.

3. Season to taste with salt and pepper. Add lime juice, toss, and serve.

Tomato Pudding

Although a vegetable "pudding" may sound odd, this is an old family recipe and a favorite of my husband's. These days I usually use whole-grain bread instead of white.

Makes 6 servings

½ cup butter (1 stick)

⅓ cup finely chopped onion

⅓ cup firmly packed brown sugar

1 teaspoon salt

1 teaspoon freshly ground white pepper

2 (14.5-inch) cans stewed tomatoes, undrained

4 slices bread, toasted and cubed

1. Preheat oven to 325°F. Butter a 1½-quart baking dish.

2. In a nonstick skillet, melt butter over medium heat. Add onion and sauté until translucent. Add brown sugar, salt, pepper, and tomatoes.

3. Arrange bread cubes in bottom of prepared baking dish. Spoon tomato mixture over bread. Bake for 45 minutes, until tomato mixture is bubbling. Serve hot.

Snap Peas with Mint

I love the sweet crunch of sugar snap peas. Adding a touch of fresh mint in this simple sauté takes them to another level.

1 teaspoon olive oil

1 pound sugar snap peas, trimmed

5 mint leaves, sliced in thin shreds

Salt

1. In a skillet, heat oil over medium heat. Add snap peas and sauté for 2 minutes. Add mint and sauté another minute. Season to taste with salt and serve.

Oven-Roasted Cumin Cauliflower

I'm as addicted to this as I am to popcorn. Oven-roasting, which caramelizes the cauliflower, is the secret.

1 large cauliflower (about 2 pounds), cut into 2-inch florets

¼ cup olive oil

1 tablespoon fresh lemon juice

1 teaspoon ground cumin

½ teaspoon salt

Freshly ground white pepper

1. Preheat oven to 425° F. Line a roasting pan with parchment paper, nonstick foil, or a silicone baking mat.

2. In the roasting pan, toss cauliflower with the oil, lemon juice, and cumin. Roast until tender and caramelized, turning once, about 30 minutes.

3. Season to taste with salt and white pepper and serve.

Two-Potato Scallop

If you like scalloped potatoes, you'll enjoy the addition of yams, which are both colorful and nutritious.

Makes 4 to 6 servings

¾ teaspoon ground nutmeg

2 teaspoons salt

¾ teaspoon freshly ground black pepper

3 medium yams, peeled and thinly sliced

3 large potatoes, peeled and thinly sliced

3 tablespoons butter, cut into small pieces

2 cups heavy whipping cream

½ cup milk

1. Preheat oven to 350°F. Butter a large baking dish.

2. In a small bowl, mix nutmeg, salt, and pepper.

3. Layer both kinds of potatoes in pan, sprinkling each layer with some of the salt mixture and dotting with butter. Pour cream and milk over potatoes, pressing down gently with a spatula so that potatoes are covered in liquid.

4. Cover with foil and bake about 1¼ hours, or until potatoes are tender.

5. Remove foil. Turn oven to broil. Broil potatoes until browned, about 3 minutes. Allow to rest for 5 minutes before serving.

Creamy Colcannon

Colcannon is a traditional Irish dish of mashed potatoes and cabbage. This version gets an added flavor boost with bacon and cheese.

Makes 8 servings

2 pounds potatoes, peeled and cubed

6 tablespoons butter, divided

1 cup chopped red onion

6 cups finely shredded green cabbage

¾ cup milk

¾ teaspoon salt

3 strips bacon, cooked crisp and crumbled

1 cup coarsely grated sharp cheddar or Kerrygold
    Dubliner cheese

Freshly ground black pepper

1. Cook potatoes in boiling water until tender, about 20 minutes.

2. Meanwhile, in a large skillet with lid, melt 5 tablespoons butter over medium heat. Add onion and cook for 5 minutes, stirring occasionally, until soft. Add cabbage, cover, and cook for 5 minutes, until wilted.

3. Drain potatoes; add milk and salt and mash. Add cabbage mixture, crumbled bacon, and

cheese, and season to taste with pepper. Transfer to a serving bowl, top with remaining tablespoon butter, and serve.

Sausage and Vegetable Strata, page 182

Apple Sausage Balls, page 183

Crab Cakes Benedict, page 196

Honey Citrus Fruit, page 197

Breakfast

Stuffed Cinnamon Raisin Toast

This French toast has a creamy layer hidden inside. If you prefer, substitute your favorite bread for the cinnamon raisin bread.

Makes 4 servings

1 (8-ounce) package neufchâtel or reduced-fat cream cheese, chilled

¼ cup powdered sugar

8 slices cinnamon raisin bread

3 large eggs, beaten

½ cup half-and-half

¼ cup butter

Maple syrup, warmed, for serving

1 pint fresh strawberries, hulled and halved

1. In a medium bowl, combine neufchâtel and powdered sugar; mix well. Spread onto 4 bread slices. Top with the remaining bread slices, forming sandwiches.

2. In a pie pan, add eggs and half-and-half; mix well.

3. In a large skillet, melt the butter over medium heat. Dip sandwiches in the egg mixture, coating both sides well. Cook 2 minutes on each side, until golden.

4. Slice each sandwich in half diagonally. To serve, drizzle with maple syrup and top with strawberries.

Cheddar-Sausage Brunch Muffins

These "muffins" go together quickly, but if you want to make it even easier, precook the sausage the night before.

Makes 4 servings

½ pound breakfast sausage

¾ cup all-purpose flour

1 teaspoon baking powder

¼ teaspoon salt

1 tablespoon butter, melted

1 teaspoon Dijon mustard

½ cup milk

½ teaspoon cayenne pepper

⅓ cup chopped green onions

½ cup coarsely grated sharp cheddar cheese

1. Preheat oven to 400°F. Grease a mini muffin pan.

2. In a skillet, brown sausage over medium heat, stirring to crumble; drain well.

3. In a large bowl, combine flour, baking powder, salt, melted butter, and mustard. Add milk and mix. Stir in the sausage, cayenne, green onions, and cheese (mixture will be thick). Spoon into prepared mini muffin pan, filling cups two-thirds full. Bake 12 to 14 minutes, until golden. Remove from pan immediately and serve warm.

Sausage and Vegetable Strata

This one-dish meal is a crowd pleaser, perfect for breakfast or brunch. Be sure to allow the strata to sit for at least one hour before baking to allow the bread to soak up the custard.

Makes 4 to 6 servings

1 pound breakfast sausage
1½ tablespoons olive oil
½ cup trimmed and sliced (2-inch) fresh asparagus
½ cup sliced fresh mushrooms
½ cup cored and diced red bell pepper
1 cup coarsely grated cheddar cheese
½ cup diced zucchini
10 large eggs
1 pint half-and-half (2 cups)

2 tablespoons Dijon mustard
Salt and freshly ground black pepper
4 slices bread, cubed
½ cup chopped green onions

1. Spray a 9-by-13-inch pan with nonstick cooking spray.

2. In a large skillet, brown sausage over medium heat, stirring to crumble. Drain well and set aside.

3. In the same skillet, heat oil over medium heat and sauté asparagus, mushrooms, bell pepper, and zucchini until just tender.

4. In a large bowl, add eggs, half-and-half, mustard, and salt and pepper to taste; whisk until smooth.

5. Line bottom of prepared pan with half of the bread cubes. Scatter half of the sausage, vegetables, green onions, and cheese over bread. Repeat with remaining bread, sausage, vegetables, cheese and green onions. Pour egg mixture evenly over top. Refrigerate for at least 1 hour, or up to overnight.

6. Bake in preheated 350°F-oven until eggs are just set, about 1 hour. Let stand for 8 to 10 minutes before serving.

Apple Sausage Balls

When I was young, my mom made sausage balls for my brother and me. We loved them. While they make a great breakfast (try serving them with fresh fruit and muffins), they're also a wonderful appetizer.

⅔ cup peeled, cored, and coarsely grated fresh
   apple (such as Granny Smith)

1 pound breakfast sausage

1½ teaspoons baking soda

2 cups coarsely grated cheddar cheese

¾ cup all-purpose flour

½ teaspoon ground cinnamon

1 tablespoon butter, melted

¼ cup pecans, toasted and chopped

1. Preheat oven to 375°F.

2. In a large mixing bowl, combine apple, sausage, baking soda, cheese, flour, cinnamon, butter, and toasted nuts; stir well. Form into 1-inch balls and place on a rimmed, ungreased baking sheet.

3. Bake 18 to 20 minutes or until golden brown. Cool 2 minutes before removing sausage balls from pan. Serve warm.

BREAKFAST

Vegetable Frittata

Breakfast, brunch or dinner, this dish always satisfies.
Serve it hot for a delicious, veggie-packed meal.

Makes 4 to 6 servings

3 tablespoons olive oil

1½ cups chopped zucchini

1½ cups sliced fresh mushrooms

¾ cup chopped onion

¾ cup cored and chopped green bell pepper

1 clove garlic, minced

8 large eggs, beaten

¼ cup half-and-half

1 (8-ounce) package neufchâtel or reduced-fat cream
    cheese, softened

2 cups coarsely grated swiss cheese

4 slices whole-wheat bread, cubed

1 teaspoon salt

¼ teaspoon freshly ground black pepper

1. Preheat oven to 350°F. Spray a 9-by-13-inch baking dish with nonstick cooking spray.

2. In a large skillet, heat oil over medium heat. Add zucchini, mushrooms, onion, bell pepper and garlic; sauté until tender. Remove from heat and let cool slightly.

3. In a large bowl, beat together the eggs and half-and-half. Stir in cream cheese, swiss cheese, bread cubes, and sautéed vegetables. Add salt and pepper, mix well, and pour into prepared baking dish.

4. Bake for 1 hour, or until center is set. Allow frittata to sit for 5 minutes before serving.

Huevos Rancheros

Classic huevos rancheros don't usually call for bacon, but here it gives the dish a savory boost. This version is also quick and a great option for breakfast or brunch.

2 tablespoons olive oil

4 (6-inch) corn tortillas

1 cup refried beans

½ teaspoon chili powder

½ teaspoon ground cumin

2 tablespoons canned diced fire-roasted green chilies

4 large eggs

Salt and freshly ground black pepper

1 cup coarsely grated queso cheese

8 slices bacon, cooked and crumbled

½ cup fresh salsa

1. In a large skillet, heat oil over medium heat. Fry tortillas one at a time until firm but not browned. Drain on paper towels, keeping oil in skillet.

2. Meanwhile, in a small saucepan, heat refried beans, chili powder, cumin, and green chilies over medium heat and keep warm.

3. Add more oil to skillet if tortillas have absorbed it all. Return to medium heat, add eggs, and fry until done to your liking.

4. Divide tortillas among four plates and spread each with a layer of beans. Top with cheese, fried egg, salt and pepper to taste, crumbled bacon, and salsa, and serve.

BREAKAST

Streusel Coffee Cake

Here's how to make your own beautiful and delicious coffee cake. Slicing it reveals the sweet streusel in the center.

Makes 1 (8" square) cake

2 cups all-purpose flour, divided

¾ cup sugar

¾ teaspoon salt

2½ teaspoons baking powder

¼ cup vegetable shortening

¾ cup milk

1 large egg

½ cup chopped pecans

½ cup firmly packed brown sugar

¼ cup butter, melted

1 teaspoon ground cinnamon

½ teaspoon ground nutmeg

1. Preheat oven to 375°F. Grease an 8-inch-square pan.

2. In a large bowl, combine 1½ cups flour, sugar, salt, baking powder, shortening, milk, and egg; stir just until combined. Add half the mixture to the prepared pan.

3. In a separate bowl, make a streusel by mixing together remaining ½ cup flour with pecans, brown sugar, butter, cinnamon, and nutmeg. Spoon streusel mixture on top of batter in the pan. Top with the remaining batter. Bake for 25 to 30 minutes or until wooden pick inserted in center comes out clean.

Mixed Fruit Yogurt Parfaits

This is fun to make with children and also makes an elegant breakfast for guests. Use whatever fresh fruit you prefer.

¾ cup fresh mixed fruit, sliced (try melon, berries, and kiwi)

¾ cup fresh blueberries

2 (6-ounce) containers plain yogurt

2 teaspoons honey

2 tablespoons dried shredded coconut, toasted

1 banana, peeled and sliced

⅓ cup granola

1. In four individual parfait glasses, layer the mixed fruit, blueberries, yogurt, honey, toasted coconut, banana, and granola; repeat layers as necessary until glasses are full.

BREAKAST

Spinach and Feta Bundt Quiche

Who knew that a Bundt pan could transform a quiche into a stunning presentation? And you can't go wrong combining spinach and feta.

1 (10-ounce) package frozen chopped spinach, thawed and well drained

4 ounces feta cheese, crumbled (1 cup)

½ cup finely grated parmesan cheese

¼ cup dried bread crumbs

1 bunch green onions, chopped

¼ cup minced fresh Italian (flat-leaf) parsley

½ teaspoon freshly ground black pepper

Pinch ground nutmeg

½ cup coarsely grated cheddar cheese

16 large eggs

¾ cup half-and-half

1. Preheat oven to 375°F.

2. In a large mixing bowl, combine spinach, feta, parmesan, bread crumbs, green onions, parsley, pepper, and nutmeg; blend well.

3. Grease a 12-cup Bundt pan and add cheddar cheese. Spoon spinach mixture evenly over top of cheese.

4. In a separate bowl, beat eggs and mix in half-and-half. Pour a portion of this mixture over spinach mixture, allowing spinach to absorb liquid before adding remainder.

5. Bake about 45 minutes, until firm. Invert onto serving platter and serve warm.

BREAKAST

Avocado Eggs Benedict with Lemon-Yogurt Sauce

Creamy avocados and a yogurt sauce stand in for the usual Hollandaise and make this a refreshing new breakfast solution.

⅓ cup plain Greek yogurt (low-fat or full-fat)

1 teaspoon milk

1 tablespoon lemon juice

Pinch cayenne pepper

Salt and freshly ground black pepper

4 large eggs

2 whole-wheat English muffins, split

1 large avocado, pitted, peeled, and sliced

4 slices Canadian bacon

1. In a small bowl, combine yogurt, milk, lemon juice, cayenne, and salt and pepper to taste. Mix well and set aside.

2. Using an egg poaching pan, butter the cups, add eggs and poach over simmering water to desired doneness.

3. Meanwhile, toast English muffin halves. Top each muffin half with a Canadian bacon slice and a poached egg. Fan avocado slices over eggs, season with salt and pepper to taste, and ladle sauce over the top.

BREAKAST

Crab Cakes Benedict

Most people typically eat crab at lunch or dinner. But when you substitute crab cakes for the Canadian bacon in eggs Benedict, you create a truly special breakfast. The crab cakes can certainly be enjoyed at any meal.

Makes 4 servings

Crab cakes:

1 cup crushed saltine crackers

1 cup mayonnaise (preferably a brand made with olive oil)

2 tablespoons chopped fresh basil

1 teaspoon stone-ground mustard

¼ cup chopped onion

1 stalk celery, chopped

½ lime, juiced

1 teaspoon Old Bay seasoning

Salt and freshly ground black pepper

1 pound shelled crab meat

Hollandaise sauce:

2 large egg yolks

2 tablespoons fresh lemon juice

1 teaspoon water

¼ teaspoon salt

Dash cayenne pepper

½ cup butter (1 stick), melted

To assemble:

8 large eggs

4 English muffins, split and lightly toasted

4 slices fresh tomato

Fresh parsley, for garnish

To make crab cakes:

1. Preheat oven to broil. Lightly grease a baking sheet.

2. In a large bowl, mix crushed saltines, mayonnaise, basil, mustard, onion, celery, lime juice, Old Bay seasoning, and salt and pepper to taste. Gently stir in the crab meat. Shape into 8 patties. Place on prepared baking sheet. Broil crab cakes 5 to 6 minutes on each side, or until golden brown. Keep crab cakes warm in oven while you prepare the sauce and eggs.

To make sauce:

1. In a saucepan over medium-low heat, combine egg yolks, lemon juice, 1 teaspoon water, salt, and cayenne. Whisk constantly until bubbles appear and mixture begins to thicken. Scrape mixture into blender. Slowly add melted butter as you blend the mixture; continue to blend until sauce thickens, about 30 seconds.

To assemble:

1. Using an egg poaching pan, butter the cups, add the eggs and poach over simmering water to desired doneness.

2. Place two muffin halves, cut-side up, on each plate. On each muffin half, place a tomato slice, a crab cake and then a poached egg. Spoon hollandaise sauce over each egg. Garnish with parsley and serve.

Honey Citrus Fruit

A honey-lime dressing takes fruit salad to a new level.
Use your favorite fruits and watch your family devour it.

Makes 4 servings

⅓ cup honey

2 limes

2 bananas, peeled and sliced

½ papaya, peeled and cubed

½ cantaloupe, peeled and cubed

½ cup peeled and cubed fresh pineapple

2 apples, peeled, cored, and cubed

1. Add honey to a small microwave-safe bowl and heat on high for 5 seconds.

2. Finely grate the zest of the limes, then juice them, discarding the seeds. Whisk the lime juice and half of the zest into the honey.

3. Place all fruit in a large glass bowl. Toss gently with honey-lime mixture and chill until ready to serve. At serving time, top with remaining lime zest.

Apple Steel-Cut Oatmeal

Apples add natural sweetness and creaminess to oatmeal, so there's no need for sugar or milk. Once you try this, you'll never look back.

Makes 4 servings

4 cups apple juice

2 apples, cored and chopped

1 cup steel-cut oatmeal

1 teaspoon ground cinnamon

Dried fruit of your choice, for serving

1. In a medium saucepan, combine apple juice and apples. Bring to a boil and stir in oatmeal and cinnamon. Return to a boil, then reduce heat to low, cover, and simmer 20 to 25 minutes. Serve in bowls, topped with your choice of dried fruit.

Fruit and Yogurt Smoothie

This smoothie makes a perfect breakfast, but it's also a great way to end a meal, or provide a mid-day refresher.

3 ice cubes

1 large banana, peeled and cut into 1-inch slices

1 cup fresh blueberries or raspberries

¾ cup plain yogurt

2 tablespoons honey

1. In a blender, add ice, fruit, yogurt and honey; purée for 2 minutes or until smooth.

BREAKAST

Lemon Curd-Coconut Trifle, page 208

Grilled Pineapple, page 209

Dark Chocolate Truffles, page 212

Galaktobouriko, page 213

Desserts

Citrus and Spice Poached Pears

This elegant dessert is sweet and slightly spicy. I especially love the way the little shreds of orange and lemon zest pop with flavor with each bite.

Makes 4 servings

4 firm-ripe pears (such as Bartlett or Bosc)

1 cup dry white wine

1 cup water

½ cup sugar

1 tablespoon slivered lemon zest

1 tablespoon slivered orange zest

3 tablespoons fresh lemon juice

3 tablespoons fresh orange juice

2 whole cloves

2 cinnamon sticks

2 tablespoons peeled and finely grated fresh ginger

6 whole peppercorns

1 vanilla bean

1. Peel pears leaving an inch of skin around the stems.

2. In a saucepan, combine the wine, water, sugar, citrus zest and juice, cloves, cinnamon sticks, ginger, peppercorns, and vanilla bean. Bring to a boil, add pears, then reduce heat to a simmer and cook for 15 minutes, until pears are tender. If pears aren't completely covered with liquid, turn frequently to poach evenly.

3. Remove pears from liquid and set aside. Reduce liquid in saucepan over high heat until you have about 1 cup. Return pears to liquid and let cool.

4. Just before serving, heat pears in sauce. Serve with some of the sauce spooned over the tops of the pears, making sure to include a few pieces of zest.

DESSERTS

Chocolate-Drizzled Coconut Macaroons

I grew up making coconut macaroons with Mom. Drizzling them with dark chocolate takes them over the top.

Makes 2 dozen cookies

14 ounces dried sweetened shredded coconut

1 (14-ounce) can sweetened condensed milk

1 teaspoon vanilla extract

2 large egg whites, at room temperature

¼ teaspoon salt

3 ounces semisweet or bittersweet chocolate

1. Preheat oven to 325°F. Line two baking sheets with parchment paper.

2. In a large bowl, combine the coconut, condensed milk, and vanilla.

3. In a separate bowl, using an electric stand mixer fitted with the whisk attachment, whip the egg whites and salt on high speed until they hold medium-firm peaks. Carefully fold the egg whites into the coconut mixture.

4. Drop the batter onto prepared baking sheets using a small ice cream scoop or two teaspoons. Bake for 25 to 30 minutes, until golden brown. Remove from oven, slide parchment paper off baking sheets and allow macaroons to cool.

5. Melt chocolate in a double boiler. Drizzle chocolate over macaroons with a slotted spoon. Allow chocolate to set up for a few minutes before serving or storing in an airtight container.

Lemon Syllabub

Serve this creamy dessert in parfait glasses or layer it with pound cake and fresh blueberries.

Makes 4 servings

1 cup heavy whipping cream, chilled

½ cup sugar

¼ cup dry white wine

2 tablespoons fresh lemon juice

1 teaspoon finely grated lemon zest

¼ teaspoon ground nutmeg, for garnish

Fresh mint leaves, for garnish

Lemon slices, for garnish

1. In a chilled bowl, using an electric mixer, whip the cream and sugar until the mixture begins to thicken. Gradually beat in the wine, lemon juice, and lemon zest. Continue to beat until light and fluffy. Be careful not to overbeat or mixture will turn grainy. Cover the bowl and chill until serving time.

2. Serve in chilled parfait glasses, garnished with a dash of nutmeg, sprig of mint, and slice of lemon.

DESSERTS

Fresh Cherry Crisp

There's no better way to enjoy peak-of-the-season cherries than in this delicious crisp, with rich brown sugar and a hint of nutmeg.

Makes 6 servings

½ cup all-purpose flour

1 cup old-fashioned or quick-cooking oatmeal

½ teaspoon ground cinnamon

½ teaspoon ground nutmeg

½ cup firmly packed brown sugar

½ cup butter (1 stick), at room temperature

4 cups fresh sweet cherries, pitted

1 tablespoon apple juice

¼ cup sugar

1 tablespoon cornstarch

1. Preheat oven to 375°F.

2. In a large bowl, combine flour, oatmeal, cinnamon, nutmeg, and brown sugar. Cut butter into mixture until crumbly.

3. In a separate large bowl, mix together cherries, apple juice, sugar, and cornstarch. Pour into an 8-inch-square baking pan or individual 4½ inch ramekins.

4. Bake for 30 minutes or until cherries are tender and juices are bubbly and thickened.

DESSERTS

Lemon Curd-Coconut Trifle

This is an elegant dessert with a big "wow" factor, and my friends often ask for the recipe. The trifle is simple to make and—as my niece, Lily, can tell you—it's kid-friendly, too.

Makes 4 to 6 servings

2 pints fresh strawberries, hulled
¾ cup dried sweetened shredded coconut
2 cups plain Greek yogurt (low-fat or full-fat)
2 tablespoons honey
1 (10-ounce) jar lemon curd
1 lemon, juiced and zest finely grated
1 angel food cake (9-inch), cut into 2-inch cubes

1. Preheat oven to 325°F.

2. Set aside a few whole strawberries for garnish. Cut remaining strawberries in half and set aside.

3. Spread coconut on a baking sheet and toast in the oven until just browned, about 4 minutes. Set aside.

4. In a medium bowl, combine yogurt, honey, lemon curd, lemon juice, and grated zest; stir until combined.

5. In a trifle bowl or deep glass dish, layer half the cake pieces, half the yogurt/lemon curd mixture, half the halved strawberries, and sprinkle with some toasted coconut. Repeat layers. Garnish with remaining toasted coconut and whole strawberries.

Grilled Pineapple

Sweet pineapple caramelizes on the grill. Serve with ice cream for a perfect summer dessert.

Makes as much
as desired

Fresh pineapple, peeled, cored and cut into
    ½-inch-thick slices
Olive Oil
Vanilla ice cream, for serving

1. Preheat grill to medium.

2. Just before grilling, lightly brush pineapple slices with olive oil.

3. Grill pineapple for 3 to 5 minutes on each side. Serve pineapple warm with ice cream.

Honey-Ricotta Berry Puff Pastries

Puff pastry is an easy way to transform fresh berries and ricotta cheese into an elegant dessert.

Makes 8 servings

1 (17.3-ounce) package frozen puff pastry, thawed according to package directions

½ cup honey

1 tablespoon finely grated orange zest

2 (15-ounce) containers ricotta cheese

2 cups hulled and sliced fresh strawberries

1 cup fresh raspberries

2 cups fresh blueberries

Powdered sugar, for garnish

1. Preheat oven to 375°F. Line a baking sheet with parchment paper.

2. Roll one puff pastry sheet with a rolling pin to remove all creases. Cut into 4-inch squares. Place on prepared baking sheet, leaving 1 inch space between squares. Repeat with remaining sheet of pastry. Bake for 12 to 15 minutes, until golden.

3. In a large bowl, combine honey, orange zest, and ricotta; mix well.

4. In another bowl, toss strawberries, raspberries, and blueberries.

5. Split apart each pastry into two layers. Spread ricotta mixture onto bottom squares. Top with berries and add tops of puff pastry. Lightly sprinkle with powdered sugar and serve immediately.

DESSERTS

Dark Chocolate Truffles

These are so fun to make, and they're a special gift to take to a friend. You can vary the recipe by coating the truffles in unsweetened cocoa powder or toasted coconut instead of the nuts.

Makes about 32

⅓ cup heavy whipping cream
2 cups dark chocolate chips
2 tablespoons butter, cut into pieces

¾ cup finely chopped nuts (such as almonds, pecans, or pistachios)

1. In a heavy saucepan, slowly bring the cream to a simmer over medium heat. Remove from heat and stir in the chocolate and butter. Place pan over low heat and stir mixture just until chocolate has melted. Pour into bowl. Refrigerate for 20 to 25 minutes, until slightly thickened.

2. Line a baking sheet with parchment paper. Using a teaspoon, scoop chocolate and make mounds (you will roll into balls after mixture has chilled). Drop onto parchment paper. Refrigerate for another 20 minutes.

3. Place the chopped nuts in a small bowl. Using your palms, roll chocolate mixture into balls, dropping them into the bowl of nuts as you go. Shake the bowl to evenly coat the truffles with nuts. Place in a container, separating layers with fresh parchment paper. Cover tightly and refrigerate up to 2 weeks, or freeze up to 3 months.

Galaktobouriko (Greek Custard Phyllo Pie)

When I lived in Greece, there was a bakery I often walked past that sold this traditional dessert. The custard and layers of flaky phyllo pastry made it impossible to resist, which meant that my pants got tighter as the year progressed.

Makes 15 servings

2 quarts milk (8 cups)

8 large eggs

3½ cups sugar, divided

1 cup uncooked farina cereal (such as Cream of Wheat brand)

2 teaspoons vanilla extract

1 cup unsalted butter (2 sticks), melted

1 (1-pound) package frozen phyllo dough, thawed according to package directions

2 cups water

1 lemon, juiced

1 cinnamon stick

1. Preheat oven to 350°F.

2. In large saucepan, bring milk to a boil over medium-high heat. While milk is heating, add eggs and 1½ cups sugar in a large bowl and beat well. Stir in farina cereal.

3. Slowly add egg mixture to hot milk and stir constantly until mixture thickens; add vanilla. Remove from heat.

4. Brush a 10-by-15-inch pan with some of the melted butter. Place a layer of phyllo in pan, allowing dough to hang over edge of pan. Brush dough with butter. Repeat with 10 more layers of phyllo, buttering each sheet and allowing them to hang over the edge of the pan. Pour custard over the top of phyllo. Layer 10 more sheets of phyllo, buttering each as you go, and folding in the sheets from the bottom as the layers are added.

5. Cut through the top sheets of the phyllo into lengthwise, 3-inch-wide strips. Take care not to cut through the bottom layers.

6. Bake for 45 minutes to 1 hour, or until golden brown.

7. While custard is baking, prepare syrup. In saucepan combine 2 cups water, remaining 2 cups sugar, lemon juice, and cinnamon stick; bring mixture to a boil. After syrup has come to a boil, remove from heat and remove cinnamon stick.

8. After custard has cooled a bit, cut along the same lengthwise lines you scored before baking, this time cutting through all the layers of phyllo. Cut crosswise into individual portions. Pour the warm syrup over the dessert. Serve at room temperature, and refrigerate any leftovers.

DESSERTS

Lemongrass Lemon Bars

Lemon bars have been around forever, but adding lemongrass makes them exotic and amazing.

Makes 24 bars

1 cup butter (2 sticks), plus 1 tablespoon, at room temperature, divided

2½ cups all-purpose flour, divided

¾ cup powdered sugar, plus more for garnish

½ teaspoon salt

6 large eggs

2¼ cups sugar

1¼ cups fresh lemon juice

2½ tablespoons finely grated fresh lemongrass

1. Preheat oven to 350°F. Grease a 9-by-13-inch pan with 1 tablespoon butter.

2. In a large bowl, add 2 cups flour, ¾ cup powdered sugar and the salt; mix well. Add remaining 1 cup butter and blend with a pastry cutter. Firmly press dough into pan. Bake 20 minutes, then remove crust from oven. Reduce oven temperature to 325°F.

3. Meanwhile, in another large bowl, whisk together eggs and sugar until smooth. Gently stir in the lemon juice and lemongrass. Stir in the remaining ½ cup flour.

4. Pour lemon mixture over the crust. Bake 30 to 35 minutes. Cool, then refrigerate for at least 30 minutes. Dust with powdered sugar and cut into bars.

DESSERTS

Ginger Peach Pie

When I added fresh ginger to my fresh peach pie, the first bite let me know that this dessert was really something special.

Makes one 9-inch pie

1 package refrigerated pie dough (2 crusts)

1 large egg, beaten

6 cups peeled, pitted, and sliced fresh peaches

2 tablespoons fresh lemon juice

¼ cup all-purpose flour

¼ cup cornstarch

½ cup sugar

½ cup firmly packed brown sugar

1 teaspoon peeled and finely grated fresh ginger

½ teaspoon ground cinnamon

¼ teaspoon salt

2 tablespoons turbinado sugar (such as Sugar In The Raw brand)

1. Preheat oven to 450°F.

2. Line the bottom and sides of a 9-inch pie pan with one of the pie crusts. Brush with some of the beaten egg.

3. In a large bowl, add the sliced peaches and sprinkle with lemon juice.

4. In a separate bowl, mix flour, cornstarch, sugar, brown sugar, ginger, cinnamon, and salt. Pour over the peaches and toss gently. Add peaches to pie pan and top with remaining pie crust; crimp edges together. Brush the remaining egg over the top and sprinkle with turbinado sugar. Cut several slits in the top crust.

5. Bake for 10 minutes, then reduce heat to 350°F. Bake another 25 to 30 minutes. If the edges brown too fast, cover them with foil. Cool slightly before serving.

Chocolate Satin Pie

Whether you top this with fresh seasonal berries or chopped nuts, the result is a lovely dessert for very little effort.

Graham cracker crust:

1½ cups graham cracker crumbs

6 tablespoons butter, melted

⅓ cup sugar

Filling:

1 (12-ounce) can evaporated milk

2 large egg yolks

1 (12-ounce) bag chocolate chips

Lightly sweetened whipped cream

¼ cup shelled pistachios, chopped, or fresh
    berries, for serving

To make crust:

1. Preheat oven to 375°F.

2. In a medium bowl, combine graham cracker crumbs, melted butter, and sugar. Blend well and press mixture into bottom and sides of a 9-inch pie pan or individual tart pans.

3. Bake for 5 to 7 minutes; remove from oven and cool before filling.

To make filling:

1. In a medium saucepan, whisk together evaporated milk and egg yolks. Heat over medium-low heat, stirring constantly, until mixture is very hot and slightly thickened; do not boil. Remove from heat; add chocolate chips and stir until completely melted and mixture is smooth.

2. Pour into crust; refrigerate 3 hours or until firm.

3. Just before serving, top with whipped cream and chopped nuts or fresh berries.

DESSERTS